YOUR TEAM IS NOT THE ISSUE

UNEARTH THE SYSTEMIC ROOTS OF TEAM DYNAMICS

TESS COPE

authors
AND CO.

CONTENTS

DEDICATION

To those that came before – without you, this would not be possible.

ACKNOWLEDGEMENTS

One of the foundational principles of the systemic approach is to honour history before you try to establish your unique footprint in your domain. I'd like to acknowledge and offer a respectful bow to the founder of this approach, Bert Hellinger. Without his dedication and leadership, none of this would be possible. Bert's work is renowned for identifying the governing principles of healthy systems, which we'll cover in Chapter 2.

His early work included the study of survivors of the Holocaust and his observations uncovered the phenomenon that unconscious patterns travel through the generations. Hellinger's core methodology, 'constellations', was introduced in the mid-1990s. This approach is designed to illuminate and interrupt, where appropriate, the hidden dynamics and unconscious patterns within a human system. Hellinger focused primarily on the family system. It was very quickly discovered that similar principles were true within the organisational realm. This methodology has been further developed and refined for the organisational context by a range of consultants around the globe, including Hunter Beaumont and Gunthard Weber.

Before we can invite others to adopt this deeper work, I strongly believe that we need to have 'gone there ourselves'. I've had the privilege of learning with many systemic teachers over the course of the past twelve years and I'd like to particularly acknowledge those who have had a profound effect on me in the context of the whole person journey I embarked upon in 2011.

In addition to facilitating my own growth and development, they have also enabled me to figure out how to integrate this approach so that it simultaneously adds real value for organisations and executive leadership teams. These teachers include but aren't limited to Judith Hemming (UK), Terry Wright (UK), Caroline Ward (UK), Jan Jacob Stam (The Netherlands) Sarah Peyton (US) and Stephan Hausner (Germany).

At some point, we need to bring our learning into action. I am incredibly and constantly grateful to those clients who have been open and receptive to the incorporation of the systemic approach as a means of adding material value to the development journey of their leadership teams. Some of my most valuable learnings have taken place within the ongoing exploration, application, and refinement process with them.

Finally, I'd also like to extend a huge thank you to those that provided input as part of my research and to my 'test readers' for their precious feedback as this book developed – your input has been invaluable.

INTRODUCTION

You have assembled the best talent, poured hours of quality thinking time into the optimum structure, and thought long and hard about your own leadership. And yet, here you are, burying your head in your hands with sheer frustration. All you are faced with is resistance, lethargy and dysfunctional behaviours that just don't make sense, whilst performance continues to dip.

What is even more frustrating is that you can't quite put your finger on the problem – it's hiding just underneath the surface. The obvious and pretty straightforward thing to do is to change individuals within the team, but that won't necessarily move the dial. And let's face it, you've probably tried that already.

Quite simply, in this ever evolving and complex world, the concept of team development needs an expanded lens, a delve 'beneath the floorboards', an ability to be at ease with complexity and a multi-dimensional approach.

We know from research undertaken during 2021/2022, via interviews with leaders of successful change initiatives across a wide range of sectors, that they attributed a significant proportion of success to the fact that they paid attention to these hidden systemic forces within the system.

Within the covers of this book, you will find examples of client stories whose challenges might sound very familiar.

- Issac, a newly appointed CEO stepped into a business that was losing market share and needed rapid digitalisation just to keep up. He had inherited a team of experienced professionals who were preoccupied with internal issues and were operating in silos.
- Archie, an experienced CEO took up the challenge of a transformation agenda in a family- owned business in the transport industry. Despite having a clearly laid out strategy the leadership team were continually being blown off course due to some of the family dynamics.
- Shivaun was promoted into the seat of the CEO. The role had been occupied for quite some time and the team were incredibly loyal and dependent on her predecessor's style of leadership. She needed to ensure she had the space to make the role her own and to lead in her own unique way.
- Anneke was promoted to the role of Global CEO. She needed to galvanise the support of her previous peers and steer the business into its next chapter without losing key members of the team, who felt that they should have been given the opportunity of the role.

- Angela, the VP of a Global Supply chain – the team could not keep up with the scale of demand in a high potential region. No matter how much she spent on expensive consultancy and operational fixes, another part of the supply chain would break down.
- Geraldine was recruited from within the organisation to command a business turnaround of one of the core divisions. She knew what she needed to do but was struggling to find her place in the leadership team. It was influencing the overall team dynamic, and questions were emerging on the leader's decision to appoint her.

This book sets out to provide you with a new set of lenses and frameworks that will help you get to the root cause of the dysfunction in your team and get them back on track in terms of energy, engagement and ultimately, performance.

The systemic methodology includes guidance on the care, precision, courage, and confidence to go beyond the surface layers and expose the hidden tension and dynamics so that they can be seen and ultimately, transformed.

The aim is to equip you with different questions and to support you to stay curious and keep delving beneath the layers. Real examples and frameworks will help move you closer to finding out what needs to be revealed to create movement, and ultimately enabling your team to deliver or exceed your expectations.

We will unpack real examples of work with leadership teams from global, national, and regional businesses where there has been significant business impact – these include moving the dial on quality in a high-volume, high-value business (by six percentage points), improving the service to customers from 35% to 88% and reducing staff turnover from 40% to 4%.

Examples are included from the full spectrum in terms of scale ranging from 100 employees to 100,000+. Experience has been drawn from working with a mix of start-ups, medium-sized corporates, family-owned businesses, government think tanks and public sector organisations. As you can imagine, I have utilised some creative license and anonymised all examples to protect confidentiality.

The book has been divided into four parts:

Part one provides you with underpinning philosophies and methodologies relating to the systemic approach.

Part two offers guidance on setting your team up for success during the formative stages.

Part three equips you to look underneath the floorboards and identify the root causes when the storm is brewing and the tension builds.

Part four invites you to pause and look within at your own leadership. Neglect this at your peril. As the book title suggests, it just might be true that your team is NOT the issue.

May I encourage you to dip into each section but to also complete all sections as you will find examples that will spark your reflections throughout. The early chapters give you a solid ground and the latter stages provide you with the tools and some practical application.

We finish with some final percolations to support your journaling – a highly recommended leadership practice. These are specifically included to support your reflection from a leadership perspective, but you may also find it helpful to bring these questions to the team, within your development sessions.

Throughout the book, I invite you to make the most of a wide range of resources and frameworks. Utilise what resonates, feel free to develop them and make them your own.

I believe this meets the essential ingredient of a shared context – no need for further meanderings, let's get into it...

PART 1

THE SYSTEMIC APPROACH

1

WHAT DO WE MEAN BY SYSTEMIC?

 "We have experienced amazing transformation – there is a very different energy on-site, and we have significantly moved the dial on several key metrics – including quality, customer service and people turnover which has reduced from 40% to 4%!"

ANGELA, VP OF GLOBAL SUPPLY CHAIN

The Origins of This Methodology

This approach is designed to illuminate and interrupt, where appropriate, the hidden dynamics and unconscious patterns within a human system.

As mentioned in the earlier acknowledgements section, the origins of this work date back to the mid-1990s and are based on extensive hours of observation by the psychotherapist, Bert Hellinger. This included the study of survivors of the Holocaust and the realisation that trauma is carried unconsciously through the generations. This phenomenon has been further researched through extensive studies, by looking at the changes in DNA over time. Compelling evidence has been found of transgenerational epigenetic inheritance, thereby consolidating the notion that behaviours can pass from one generation to another, without any direct contact.

Hellinger focused primarily on the family system, but it was very quickly discovered that similar principles were true within the organisational realm. The methodology was initially introduced circa thirty years ago and has been further developed and refined for the organisational context by a range of consultants around the globe during this time. I've been incorporating this approach within organisations for circa ten years with significant results on the wider business and on the team itself.

It is important to bear in mind that these inherited traumas not only carry the patterns associated with the trauma itself but also carry the resilience that was formed because of being able to withstand the trauma. When delving beneath the surface layers, it is important to identify what needs to be acknowledged and what can be respectfully left behind, as well as the resources and capabilities that can be helpfully carried forward.

What Do We Mean by System?

Let's deal with some of the terminology. When we use the phrase 'system', we are simply describing an entity that brings humans together – this can be a family (the primary source of our patterns), organisations, communities, the ecosystem we operate within and if we zoom back much further, our planet.

To be effective in this era of evolving complexity and increasing ambiguity, it can be helpful to zoom back and acknowledge what is happening in the wider context. With this widened lens, we will often notice that whatever is going on in the wider ecosystem will influence what is showing up in the organisation. Equally important to note, the dynamics that are active within the leadership team are likely to be permeating throughout the organisation, both positive and otherwise.

As above, so Below

On an individual dimension, it is key to bear in mind that each of us is influenced and shaped by the systems we have lived through before we arrived in the current team. This includes our family system and the series of organisational experiences behind us.

Family patterns carry significant weight – they are the first system we live in and are shaped by. It can be helpful to bear in mind that each of your team members will unconsciously bring their own family patterns and the patterns of their heritage to the team dynamic.

Most of the time, these patterns are quietly nestled in the background but from time to time, they may make an appearance.

For example, a person who is the eldest child and has lived through the experience of being part of a single-parent family will have learned how to carry more than that which is expected of a child.

In the organisational setting, this might mean that they are predisposed to taking on more responsibility and perhaps even stepping into the role of the boss, especially when there is a vacuum of leadership. They 'step up' from a place of good intention, but this might not always go down well with the rest of their peers and, if extended over time, will be exhausting!

The metaphor of a butterfly is helpful to hold in mind. The wings are a core component but are also almost translucent. They are there, but not always fully seen or acknowledged for their beauty and uniqueness.

Each wing is made up of two parts, one larger and one smaller. The larger part of the wing represents our family system, and as mentioned above, will inform our way of showing up in the world and carry the patterns that have been imprinted in formative years. The smaller section is that of our organisational experience. This is also imprinted with many dimensions, including positive and potentially, limiting patterns.

Imagine that each person in the team has a set of wings behind them and in any meeting, there is the potential for many more systems than you realise, influencing the conversation.

What's Different About the Systemic Approach?

When we apply a systemic lens, we include within the landscape the level of energy, vitality, and capacity for movement within the system. These are the key enablers of exceptional team performance.

It involves looking beyond the surface layer of the dynamics. It is about getting 'underneath the floorboards' and identifying the root cause, the source events. This will involve acknowledging all the systems and the history associated with them, including any trauma that has not yet been processed and is potentially 'playing out' within the team dynamic.

This exploratory process is not about assigning blame to any one individual but rather, more about getting to the origin of the tension and confronting the truth. Through this process, we create space, capacity, and hope for the future and from there, the system can settle and move.

The Defining Characteristics of This Approach

There are five broad principles and philosophies that define the systemic approach:

1. Every System is Part of a Larger System.

Regardless of the size of an organisation, it will be part of a bigger ecosystem. Each team operates in the context of the wider organisation. A regional team will be influenced by the wider, perhaps global organisation. If it's a large corporate, then it forms part of and is influenced by the sector. A family-owned business, no matter the scale, is very likely to be influenced in some way by the dynamics of the family.

The classic team developmental stages of forming, storming and norming that is the precursor for high performance are still relevant. The systemic approach is complementary to this philosophy and invites you to also consider:

- What each team member brings to the team, unconsciously as well as consciously.

- The dynamics of the wider ecosystem and their potential influence on the team
- The place of the team within, and its contribution to, the wider system
- What is needed to orient the team given its place in the wider ecosystem and the beneficiaries of its work?
- The history of the team and what might not yet have been resolved.

2. Survival Mechanisms

There are three survival mechanisms simultaneously at play within every system.

The Individual Dimension

The first of these is the personal and individual dimension. As mentioned earlier, this is significantly influenced by one's family history and is on the edge of one's awareness. Most of us are aware of our behavioural patterns and how we show up in the various systems to which we belong, but we generally don't fully acknowledge the root cause or source of those behaviours.

The fundamental human need in this personal dimension is to establish a strong sense of belonging. At an individual level, we can deal with a lot of disruption, both in terms of where we're going, maybe even why we're going there, our place in the system and how we can contribute. But the thing that will destabilise us the most is if we don't have that sense of belonging,

Individuals will often sacrifice things that are important to them, for example, one of their core principles, for the sake of having a sense of belonging within the team.

The Collective Dimension

The second survival mechanism is the collective dimension of the system as a whole. This is operating just outside of our conscious awareness. The fundamental need of the collective is to maintain or regain its wholeness i.e., to ensure there is a full and accurate record of what has happened over time and all that have contributed to this in such a way that it, and they, are fully acknowledged for their contribution. Put simply, nothing from the history is conveniently deleted.

It's important to remember that that which is excluded holds the power – it is the 'elephant in the room' that no one dares to talk about. It robs essential energy that needs to be directed towards the future.

From this intention of including and remembering, the system will often sacrifice individuals for the sake of forcing the history to be seen. The system has a way of alerting you to this pattern of exclusion and will create some dysfunction that forces you to look and get more involved. We'll look at real examples of this in Chapter 8.

As you may have noticed, there is a natural tension between the conflicting needs of the individual conscience and the collective conscience. The individual perspective recognises that it is sometimes necessary to exclude things (for example, parts of ourselves) to belong, whereas the collective conscience is driving for inclusion. This interplay can create an interesting dynamic.

The Upcoming Future

The third survival mechanism relates to time and our relationship with how this evolves. This is about the evolutionary force of the upcoming future and the underlying need to be able to evolve and grow. The distinction here is about who is in the driving seat. We often create our plans based on our previous experiences and what we would like to achieve. This is an example of planning from the place of the ego.

This third dimension invites us to hold our intentions and plans a little more lightly. Rather than being in the driving seat and creating a planned future, which will be wholly informed by the conscious mind, this is more about being alert to what we don't yet know, listening to what is needed and/or what is trying to emerge and then being responsive to it.

At its essence, the systemic philosophy suggests that the upcoming future is coming towards us. It is our job to find a way to meet it and to ensure that energy can flow through to where it is needed and enable the system (and the people within it) to meet the highest potential.

This evolutionary force is also often provoking us to consider what needs to come to an end in order that this potential can be realised. It may also be signalling that the role of the team, the ways of working or the organisation itself has, in fact, come to an end so that space for the new can be created.

The evolutionary force may initially be more about a shift in the wider ecosystem that you could not have planned for but will ultimately impact your organisation and your team. A great example of this might be the arrival of the Coronavirus in 2019, which created a global and fundamental shift in how we work. With reduced air travel and an increase in people working more flexibly and often from home, there is a decreasing need for energy-draining high-rise offices. Technology is fully optimised to create connections virtually. This forced change made us think about why and when we bring our people together and is likely to have a positive impact on the planet!

This degree of transformation is not necessarily something we would have planned as a society and certainly not at the pace it happened.

3. The Overarching Principles of a Healthy System

There are three fundamental principles that need to be taken care of in facilitating and sustaining a healthy system within which people and teams thrive and can ultimately deliver their optimum performance.

I will refer to these as 'The 3 x O's'. These provide a helpful set of systemic lenses through which you can get below the surface layers of dysfunctional behaviours and patterns.

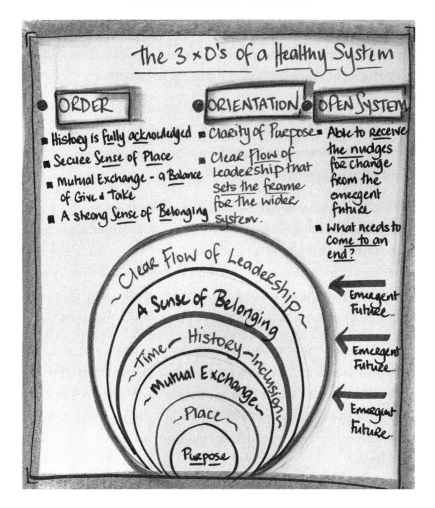

Order

A sense of calm and order is facilitated when there is an acknowledgement of all that has happened and all those who have made significant contributions are included. When we know the history that lies behind us, it provides reassurance and solid grounding upon which people can stand. When there is solid ground and a sense of why we are here to orient us (see notes on orientation below), then we can take our place within the system and understand how we can make our contribution to the team, organisation and ultimately, to customers.

Within a family system, we have a secure and consistent sense of place. We will always be the first, second or third child – we understand where we fit, regardless of the unique makeup of the family. It is undeniable.

Within an organisational context, however, our sense of place is conditional upon making a consistent contribution to purpose. This is just as relevant at an individual level as it is for teams and functions. If individuals are making a consistent and appropriate contribution to the purpose and priorities of the team, they have a right to a secure and clear sense of place within the team.

There needs to be a sense of mutuality – a balance of give and take between team members and between the team and the parts of the organisation they interact with. Mutuality is vitally important for the organisation as a whole and, how it contributes to your consumers/customers and the wider ecosystem.

If this does not feel balanced, over time it will show up in various ways including a decline in energy and employee engagement, reduced efficiency, a decay in cross-department relations and from a market perspective, a drop in sales. It is unlikely that this phenomenon will be explicitly called out – it is more of an underlying and implicit expectation that sits in the unconscious mind but when neglected, will show itself.

When each of these ordering principles is established, that fundamental survival mechanism of the individual - to belong -

is made easier. This need to belong is as relevant to each employee as it is to the team and to the company that sits within a wider group of companies.

This combination of aspects can be particularly tricky when you have an organisation that has been through a variety of mergers and acquisitions, and you have team members coming together from different parts. It's a bit like a blended family scenario when the original parents split, find new partners, and bring their respective children together into one new family unit.

At the simplest level, the history and contribution of each organisation that has made up the current organisation deserves to be given a place in the narrative and by doing so, you can create a clear and secure sense of place and the foundation for mutuality for the current team members.

Orientation

A sense of orientation anchors the energy and provides direction in a team – it enables momentum and provides a compass and a process that enables evaluation and course correction. Orientation in this context has two key components.

Clarity of Purpose

This includes the creation and clear communication of purpose, vision and being explicit about whom the team and organisation are serving.

Clear Flow of Leadership

This highlights the importance of clarity, consistency and understanding of where decisions are made, creating room for co-creation and a healthy dose of empowerment. The system and the people within it have enough of a container to provide focus and enough space to move autonomously.

Openness

To progress and thrive, a system needs to remain open. Its boundaries need to be permeable enough to be able to notice the impulses for change coming from customers, the sector, and the wider context. The system needs to have the capacity to evolve and flow. A system with solid boundaries that tries to maintain the status quo will only shrivel and die in today's fast-moving society.

In summary, when these essentials of order, orientation and openness are incorporated, energy flows and performance follows.

4. The Mindset Required - problems are often solutions in disguise

It is important to pause and reflect when exploring issues in the team. It can be very helpful to reframe problems from a systemic perspective. Rather than being recruited into the mentality of solving issues, or immediately trying to allocate the responsibility to the appropriate team member, we are invited to pause and ask ourselves what is really going on.

Keep your mind alert to the fact that the collective consciousness of the system is always seeking to be accurate and complete, and may be trying to communicate something important, including the disruption of one of the layers within the 3 x O's framework above. This dysfunction within the team may simply be a message and the individual who is caught up in these dysfunctional behaviours might merely be the messenger.

Within the family setting, it is often said that children are the symptom bearers of what lies unresolved in the parents. We are working with the same principle here.

Put simply, the dysfunction or disruption in the team has a function – it might be trying to communicate a deeper problem. When something is missing or excluded from the narrative, the system will find a way to bring this to the attention of the incumbents. This is not always a conscious choice or a pleasant experience!

More specifically, repeating issues and patterns are often signals that some of the more fundamental principles, such as place, inclusion (history), exchange and belonging, have been disrupted. This might be in the current context, but it might also be further back in time and as yet, unacknowledged, and unresolved.

By acknowledging that problems might be a solution for something much more fundamental, we can suspend our judgement and are more likely to identify the root cause and ultimately enable the return of energy, vitality, and healthy relationships.

5. The Methodology

The systemic approach is ultimately aiming to facilitate two key movements for a team:

- Surface and release the limiting patterns.
- Free up the team to move towards its highest potential.

The methodology has been designed to uncover and magnify the dynamics and unconscious patterns so that they can be seen, acknowledged, and understood.

The systemic approach requires you to go beyond the logical and analytical and to work at the opposite end of the spectrum, i.e., to work with what is not necessarily seen or tangible in the first instance. It is not about working in straight lines and requires a new mode of listening – you can read a bit more on this within the next section.

This process may take some time, it is not a 'quick fix' solution. It is about unlocking new layers and facilitating new, and often game-changing, insights.

One of the ways in which we bring this clarity and alternative perspective to the surface is via a 3D mapping process. Within the map we are looking to expose the connections, lack of connection and the hidden architecture of the team and its environment. We are aiming to unpack the hidden layers, the areas that have become entangled, stuck, or toxic, and ultimately, to reveal the root cause and the source events.

It's about looking for repeating patterns and getting to the source of these patterns. To do that, you need to cultivate a special attitude of seeing. Instead of zooming in, you need to zoom out to see the team in the context of their organisation and the system as a whole.

On most occasions, it is super helpful to go back in time, potentially as far back as the founders or at least back to the time and reason the team was formed. Depending on the level of the team you are working with, you may need to zoom out to the external environment and the societal context. e.g., what was happening in society at the time this organisation was formed? What was the very good reason this organisation came into being when it did? What was its purpose at that point in time?

By appropriately adjusting the map and introducing the appropriate interventions, you will be able to identify and work with the root causes and release the entanglements that will enable the team, the system, and those within it, to settle. This combination of precise and spacious steps enables the movements mentioned above.

A New Mode of Listening

The way of tuning into and listening to the organisation as a whole, dynamic system is different from our 'classic mode' of listening. We take off the blinkers and adjust our antennae so that we can take in a widened range of information – the tangible and the less tangible. We pay attention to our gut reactions, the nudges and the whispers that are so delicate that we might need to lean in to hear them.

We work with the 'felt sense', the visceral experience and your intuition as it emerges. We give credibility to this extensive flow of data in a way that we might not normally do within the classic business context.

Your felt sense is so much more powerful than you might realise. Circa 80% of the fibres in the vagus nerve (the longest nerve in the autonomic nervous system of the human body) runs from the body up to the brain – not the other way around. Our nervous system is constantly scanning for data and, for safety.

Our systems are finely tuned to pick up signals from others and, to be able to read the state of their nervous system. In summary, we are picking up a wealth of information that is being channelled through our bodies, if we can train ourselves to listen.

This approach invites us to hold the premise that what we experience on a visceral level can be viewed as potentially crucial insight into what is going on for the individual, in the team, organisation, or the wider ecosystem. Rather than dismiss these glimpses, nudges, images, and intuitions – the suggestion is to pause and explore them.

However, when we work in this way, we need to be careful not to open dimensions that are outside the domain of the team. When working with a divisional leadership team for example, it would not be appropriate to open and critique the remit of the next level up, i.e., the global leadership team. If we do so, then we are 'parentifying' the team and creating an unhealthy dynamic of becoming too big, which can show up as arrogance and cynicism.

Summary

There's a lot in this chapter, so let's just summarise the critical headlines:

- The overarching objective of the systemic approach is to facilitate a sustainable movement for the team toward their purpose, their vision and in service of their 'customers' (whomever they may be). When this is the case, there is likely to be a higher level of energy, vibrancy, and vitality in the system – all of which facilitate the realisation of potential and ultimately, enable exceptional performance.

- Where this vitality and movement is not the current reality, the systemic approach seeks to get to the root cause of the limiting patterns. The root cause and the associated dynamics are often beyond the team's conscious awareness. They will be frustrated and potentially interpret the issue as a purely relational one, often pinpointing one person at the centre of this. The truth of this stuck and/or toxic sensation eludes them.
- The systemic approach maximises the use of physical space (literally and virtually) as well as a conscious slowing of pace to unpack the dynamics so that the root cause can be fully seen, confronted, experienced, and acknowledged.
- There are five defining characteristics of a system:

1. Every system is part of a larger system.

2. There are three key principles that enable a healthy system. These include a sense of order, strong orientation and direction setting (facilitated by clarity of purpose and a clear flow of leadership) and a degree of openness so that the system can move and evolve in alignment with and in response to the upcoming future.

3. There are three survival mechanisms within the system and each of them have different fundamental needs (Individual = sense of belonging, collective = to be whole

& complete, and upcoming future = the flexibility to evolve & grow).

4. A shift in mindset is required – problems are often solutions in disguise and often signify an unmet need from another dimension of the system or an unresolved issue from your history line.

5. The methodology invites you to operate and work beyond the logical and rational part of your brain. It's important to practice an embodied means of knowing and start to increase your level of trust in your intuition about the experience.

- When you have incorporated the systemic lens as part of your strategic leadership, you will be able to shift gears between the logical and tangible and the phenomenological approaches, thereby expanding the flow of critical information from multiple dimensions.

2

WHAT DOES A HEALTHY TEAM LOOK LIKE?

Let's first acknowledge the impact you have as a leader on the climate and environment you create within the team and thus, on the wider business. Based on the extensive and robust research from Hay McBer (now called The Hay Group), we know that the way you show up has a 50-70% impact on the climate within your team and that, in turn, can have up to 28% impact on bottom line results. So, how you show up has a huge impact – it matters! It's important for you to have a deep understanding of why you might show up the way that you do, and you can read more about this in Chapter 10.

Every new team will move through a series of development stages until such time as trust is embedded and there is clarity and alignment on the why, what, and how of the task at hand. You can find out more about what you could expect to experience in each stage of the team development journey, and how to address any issues, within the remaining chapters.

Whilst the elements mentioned above are foundational, it doesn't mean they are easy - it requires strong leadership, intentionality from all team members and an investment of time. A mistake I often see with newly formed teams is that all the attention is focused on the why and the what in the assumption that by working on these together, the trust and relationship building will look after itself over time. This is naïve at best.

If we can assume that you are investing in a team that will spend at least a few years together, the investment will be worth it. By slowing down and investing in the human dimension up front, you will create the capacity to accelerate towards exceptional performance.

For this time with the team to be effective, you need to be willing to be vulnerable and to bring your full self to the conversation. It will require courage to confront any tensions you have inherited or have already started accumulating, and, to wholeheartedly listen to the feedback and requests from the team.

If you are taking on a new team, look out for the following indicators of a healthy system that you should be able to pick up pretty immediately:

- A sense of cohesion & an ease around collaboration
- High levels of energy and vitality
- Capacity and openness to move, evolve and grow.
- Strong connection with the consumer/customer
- Consistent delivery of exceptional performance
- Appetite for feedback and constant learning

If the energy is low and lethargic, it might be a signal that the team is drowning in rigid bureaucracy and processes. Perhaps the team was restructured recently, and people don't yet know each other very well. There may also be a history of churn in the team or perhaps the leadership chair was vacant for a while and the team shifted into a silo mentality as a means of survival. All of these might be true, but be aware, if you only work on these surface layers, and you haven't identified the root cause, these symptoms will persist, or at least emerge later and potentially in another form or another part of the organisation.

The systemic approach, and the 3 x O's framework, mentioned in Chapter 1, provide a very helpful lens to go a bit deeper. It will help you identify the root cause of the team dynamics and ultimately transform performance.

A Sense of Order

This sense of order encompasses many aspects but there are a few primary dimensions.

Time

In a healthy, high-performing team, all of what has happened before (and those that have contributed to it), including the founding principles, the core values, the highs, the lows and even the most painful experiences are included in the narrative. By including these aspects, you create the opportunity for the insights and learning to be built upon and to inform the onward trajectory.

This doesn't mean that you need to continue 'carrying' any limiting patterns or ways of operating that are no longer serving you or the team. In fact, the opposite is true. By respectfully acknowledging them and the role they have played up to this point, you can then leave them behind as part of the fabric of history, safe in the knowledge that they won't come back to 'bite you'.

The 'level' and remit of the team will dictate the expanse of the history that you need to include in your history map. If you are responsible for the top team, then looking at the business as a whole and its relationship with those you serve, including the external market, is important and should be included along with all the internal dimensions.

If your team is further 'in' the organisation, i.e., you are not responsible for the overall organisation, then the concept of including the history that more directly pertains to the team and the context within which it sits is more appropriate.

Within the recommended process of mapping and including your history, it is important to remember that every team is part of a bigger context. By doing so, you are more alert to the phenomenon that what happens 'above', will also influence what happens 'below'.

As above – So below

The survival mechanism of the collective, as mentioned in Chapter 1, is important to bring to the forefront here. When key people or events are excluded from the narrative, other members of the team will be 'recruited' into the vacuum, i.e., into the space of what is being excluded. In some instances, members of the team (or whole functions) can start behaving like the excluded element. This phenomenon of taking on the identity and behaviour of who or what has been excluded is called identification – you can learn more about this in Chapter 7.

It is not unusual for senior leadership to be shocked when a person or function starts behaving like the individual or function that has been exited. This survival mechanism of the collective consciousness is forcing the business and leadership to acknowledge and remember that which is missing. This does not mean that you cannot restructure your team or the business, but it does put an emphasis on the importance of robust and respectful endings. Until such time as the excluded part has been appropriately remembered and acknowledged, the system will continue to recruit other parts of the system into this vacuum.

When you can facilitate this remembering, you release that team member (or function) from unconsciously carrying this burden.

Place

When a team is firing on all cylinders, it would suggest that each team member is fully occupying their own 'spot'. They each have a clear sense of place and the contribution that is required from them, relative to their role, their function, and the overall sense of direction. They are not trying to be too big, and they are also not playing small.

The clarity of the team purpose is relevant as it helps each person find their respective place in terms of how they (and their function) contribute to the purpose and how they do this in relation to each other. Each role and function sits comfortably alongside the other and can rely on the other for what is expected. There is a sense of cohesion and interdependence.

Problems occur when members of the team operate from beyond their right place and the right size. It will not normally be a conscious decision and is often triggered by other events. An example of such an event would be the absence of the leader or when the leader is not fully occupying their 'seat'. When they are pulled away or their attention is diverted, the rest of the team will be required to take care of the business. Rather than the team stepping up as a collective force in this instance, it can sometimes trigger one (or several) of the team members to assume control. If the need for action is consciously agreed upon and made explicit within the team, this can be a highly effective interim strategy.

Often, however, this movement to take control is a less conscious act and can impact the team dynamic and remain festering beneath the surface for some time. More information on the patterns related to distortions of place can be found in Chapter 7.

Mutual Exchange

The theme around mutual exchange is self explanatory. In a high-performing team, this relates to the sense of giving and taking being in balance over time. There will always be moments when team members need to call upon each other – this is about the willingness and the follow through of reciprocation.

When there is a lack of mutual exchange within a team, it can become rigid, stuck and will often manifest in a culture of separation and silos.

This need for mutuality is applicable in every facet of the organisation, including between the organisation and with those it serves i.e., it is applied internally and externally. When the organisation is experienced as taking more than it is contributing, not only with customers but also in the value chain, it will often show up in very material ways, such as a decline in sales, revenue, and market share. In these scenarios, organisations are often enticed into the obvious solutions such as re-branding or restructuring when the underlying need is much more subtle yet profound.

Some of us tend to over give and the same is true for the bias towards taking. In both instances, this pattern normally originates in our family system.

Each team can manifest a wide range of systemic patterns throughout its developmental stages. As per the metaphor of the butterfly mentioned in Chapter 1, within any team, you will have the patterns of the organisation, and the family patterns of each team member, potentially activated at any one point in time. As is the case about all the dimensions above, it's helpful to be alert and look beyond the immediate behaviour and get to the root cause. You can learn more about surfacing the root cause in Chapter 8.

The three aspects above (time, place, and mutual exchange) do not operate in isolation of each other. They are interconnected. So, for example, if you have a new team and you are trying to help them find their place, one of the ways you can do this is to establish and clarify a few hierarchies based on time. Here are just a few examples:

- Who has been in the organisation for the longest time?

  o They will be able to offer the most knowledge and experience of the business.

- Who has the most experience in the sector?

  o They may have come from another organisation but have been in the sector overall for longer than some of the team members above.

- Who is the most qualified in a particular discipline?

  o This could be the new starter – giving them a 'higher place' in this hierarchy, despite being at the other end of the spectrum on many of the others.

By clarifying some of these nuances, you set the team up for finding their place relative to each other and invite a richer level of mutual exchange on how they can help each other contribute to the team purpose.

Belonging

The primary survival mechanism, at the individual dimension, is that of belonging. It is more important than the elements of time, place, and exchange. In times of significant disruption, including wholesale restructuring, a secure sense of belonging will ensure the team stick together.

It enables the team to be more resilient and ensures that you can hold onto your key players. When team members feel like they are standing 'shoulder to shoulder', they can withstand an inordinate amount of change, including confusion around their individual roles and transformation of their reason for being as an entity.

Keep in mind, especially during the formative stages of your team, the importance of building and maintaining genuine connection and trust. These are essential conduits towards this sense of belonging. We'll come back to the dimensions of trust and connection in Chapter 4.

In summary, the sense of belonging is the backbone upon which you build your high-performing team. It is the base of the pyramid upon which everything else can be established. Ignore it at your peril.

Orientation

Each team needs a gravitational force that ensures they are pulling in the same direction. From a systemic perspective, this includes the components of a team purpose, which acts as a lighthouse, and a clear flow of leadership.

The sense of purpose, sometimes called 'the north star', provides clarity on why the team exist i.e., what have they been brought together to do (that would not otherwise happen) and a clear flow of leadership distils the 'rules of engagement' where and how decision-making works within the team.

Each of these aspects is interdependent. Team Purpose is a contributing factor to the sense of place team members' experience mentioned above. When they understand the role of the collective, they can also find their unique place and contribution to the purpose. They will also have a sense of what they can rely on others for, thereby creating fertile ground for mutual exchange.

In an ideal world, as a leader, you will co-create and distil both aspects with your team. When there is a new context and the team doesn't currently exist, this is entirely possible. However, when you inherit a team, don't jump to the conclusion that you can't start again with a co-creative approach.

If you are the last to arrive in the team and take up the position of leader, it is prudent to first observe, listen and tune into these aspects before rushing in. Take some time and create genuine space for the history of the business and the team to be fully understood and honoured before introducing your own preferred ways of operating.

Even when your remit is to come in and reshape the business and the team within it, take some time to honour what has been before and engage the team in the process of transformation wherever possible. At some point in the process, you need to discern who is up for coming with you on the journey and who isn't.

When you have team members who aren't, create the space for healthy endings – it is an essential part of providing space for new and robust beginnings of who and what comes later. Ensure the leavers can depart with their heads held high and feel acknowledged for the contribution they have made. This mitigates triggering any unconscious resistance in the organisation and sends the message to those that remain that they need not be hijacked by 'survivor guilt'. It also transmits a very clear narrative about how all contributions are acknowledged along the journey and that there will come a time when the requirements evolve. When this happens, it will be handled with deep respect and intentionality, and for those that come later, there will be freedom to determine what is needed. We'll come back to the process of facilitating healthy endings in Chapter 5.

An Open System

When an organisation is formed, it is typically very attuned to its target market and super responsive as customers' needs change and the market evolves. When an organisation gets to a certain scale, however, it can become more focussed on what is happening inside the organisation rather than staying alert to the changing needs of those it serves.

This normally happens as a means of protecting itself from internal pressures and politics. The reality is that the organisation can end up starving itself from the stimulus and feedback from customers i.e., the energy upon which it thrives. When this flow of mutual exchange is thwarted, there is an impact on how long this imbalance can be sustained.

The lag factor in transforming the business to better meet the changing needs of customers will impact performance, limit potential, and ultimately restrict the life expectancy of the organisation.

If you are leading an external-facing team, then your challenge is to find a way for the messages of what's happening in the market to get through to the rest of the organisation and if you are an internal team, don't let your team get lost in internal politics. Keep creating opportunities for the team to pay attention to those you serve.

Be prepared to evolve your ways of working but also to transform on a more radical dimension. This might include reviewing your sense of purpose as a team.

———

Issac was appointed as the new UK CEO of a family-owned business creating a portfolio of products distributed through retail, to consumers. The organisation had international reach, was headquartered in Europe, and comprised of an amalgamation of two competing businesses, via acquisition some twelve years earlier.

Employees were extremely proud and associated themselves primarily with the brand they were working on, rather than the organisation as a whole. Everyone, regardless of their level in the business, was incredibly commercially minded and the primary metrics for most areas of the business were sales revenue and profit.

Each group of brands fought hard for their share of voice in their market and were in the top tier of products for each of the sectors they occupied. If someone had responsibility for the profit and loss then they were seen as having some influence and power in the organisation and if they were hitting their budget for revenue and the bottom line, they were gifted some autonomy.

But the business had plateaued, and sales were tumbling in some sectors. The business was very good at launching new products and although closing brands was not a well-rehearsed discipline, they had recently had to do more of this than was comfortable.

There were closely guarded pockets of digital expertise, but the organisation was significantly 'behind the curve'. Some parts of the business seemed to be holding on to the nostalgia of the 'old way of doing things. Digitalisation was a missing and crucial capability that would be required to secure the longer-term future of the business.

Isaac's predecessor had been in place for an extended period and was reported to have a command-and-control leadership style. Issac had inherited a leadership team that had, in the main, extensive experience in the sector and most of them had been in the business for a considerable number of years. They were super talented in their respective business areas/functional areas of excellence but in the absence of a coherent, joined-up strategy, had migrated into their operational silos.

There were pockets of people that knew each other well

and these relationships had been formed from within the original host organisation.

The departure of Isaac's predecessor was not expected so he was expecting to have a tough task ahead of him to get the team on board. The energy was low, the level of trust varied significantly and there were lots of frustrations aired at the coffee machine that didn't make their way to the leadership table. It would have been very easy to assume most of these characteristics were purely down to their resistance to his arrival, concern about performance and some degree of personality clashes within the team. It wasn't, and usually isn't, that straightforward!

As we unpacked the layers, we discovered a myriad of systemic issues under the floorboards. Issac needed to incorporate work on quite a few of the dimensions of a healthy system (captured in the 3 x Os mentioned earlier) to really grab hold of the business, halt the decline and have his leadership team driving the agenda with him. We'll come back to Isaac's team in Chapters 7 and 11, to dig a bit deeper into their patterns and the systemic interventions that helped release a new level of energy, coherence, and alignment.

In the meantime, here are a few percolations that might provoke your thoughts on what will help elevate your own team.

A few percolations:

Percolations are intended to support your reflections as a leader. I encourage you to spend a few minutes capturing your thoughts and ideas that emerge. If it feels right, these musings might be worth bringing to one of your team development sessions as a platform for a rich conversation.

- Is the narrative of your team fully inclusive?

  ○ Does it include the founding energy, founding principles and all the history that has got it to where it is today?
  ○ If not, what can you put in place that enriches the history map such that it includes all the key people and events that have contributed up to this stage?

- Does each member of your team have a clear and secure sense of place, such that they consistently deliver on expectations?

  ○ If not, what's missing?

- How would you rate the balance of give and take:

  ○ Between team members?
  ○ Between your team and interdependent teams?
  ○ Between the organisation and those it serves?

- How would you rate the sense of belonging in the team, where 10/10 is described as the team being at stake for each other, having each other's backs and operating as a line of one?

o If it's less than where you want it to be, take some time to reflect on what might be underneath this.
o How can you create the environment to surface this underlying issue?

- To what extent does your Team Purpose clarify the unique contribution that would not happen without the team's existence?

o To what extent have you clarified each team member's role and their contribution to this purpose – so that they can find their right place in the team?
o How can you create the conditions and readiness to have this conversation?

- When was the last time you exposed your team to feedback from your key customers?

o When was the last time you sense-checked your impact as a team?
o To what extent is your team's contribution still relevant in today's context?
o If you needed to open the team up to more stimulus from outside the organisation, what's one thing you do in the next ninety days?

3

THE KEY PRINCIPLES

The fundamental and formative work of Tuckman (1965) that identified and characterised the development stages of a team, remains relevant. Each team, regardless of its hierarchical level in the organisation, needs to move from the forming stage and navigate the storming phases to move towards high performance. This is certainly true from a relational perspective, where building trust is a critical component, as evidenced by the expansive work of Patrick Lencioni.

The systemic approach is complementary to these principles and goes broader and deeper. There is a danger that we rush to the obvious and tangible requirements of a team and avoid confronting some of the more fundamental, intangible issues that are just out of sight. In the interests of speed, it is also tempting to attribute these dynamics to individuals or to a function or division, represented by the current incumbents. The systemic approach encourages you to go beyond symptoms and work at a deeper level by undertaking some root cause analysis.

Just as children are the symptom bearers in the family system, team members are the symptom bearers of what hasn't yet been processed further up the organisation or further back in time.

It is often the case that the underlying issues driving the behavioural dynamics go beyond the current incumbents and the current context. This will require going back initially, to help the team move further forward more quickly. There is often some resistance to going back, especially from newer members of the team who might feel this process is less relevant.

As you will discover in the recommended approach later in this chapter, there is a significant level of latent energy and insight to be harvested from going back to the roots of the organisation. It often helps to surface the innate pride and heritage upon which the business was founded and can help make sense of why some things are done the way that they are. It also provides a much richer and more meaningful component of the onboarding process and will help accelerate knowledge gathering, covering in a few hours that which otherwise would have taken new starters six-twelve months to fully absorb, appreciate and understand.

The overarching aim of the systemic approach is to enable movement – the first stage of which is to unpack and release any limiting patterns, and then ultimately enable the team (and individuals within it) to move towards their highest potential.

What is a Limiting Pattern?

In this context, I refer to a pattern of behaviour that repeats, without any logic or conscious awareness of why it is that way. At face value, it is behaviour that does not support forward momentum. In fact, it is typically behaviour that forces you to stop and explore. It may be the behaviour of a member of the team or a whole function or division.

An example of a limiting pattern could be the constant churn in a particular team role. No matter how many hours you invest in the recruitment stages, you still find that after the first few months, the new person isn't working out or they decide to leave. It can't always be their fault – there's another dynamic at play. I encourage you to get curious and to delve deeper.

In each case, it is something that is happening in the here and now and on the face of it, it just doesn't make sense. Inherent limiting patterns are often due to unresolved dynamics further up in the organisation or unresolved issues sitting further back in time. As mentioned in Chapter 1, we know from scientific research that unprocessed trauma in our personal system can be carried unconsciously for up to three generations. And from the more recent experiences of this approach in the organisational domain, we have observed that there appears to be a dimension of organisational memory that resides within the organisation itself, i.e., it is not reliant on specific individuals carrying this memory on behalf of the organisation.

These unresolved issues/events are due to distortion or disruption in the fundamental principles of order, orientation and openness referenced in chapters 1 and 2.

Be careful, however, not to oversimplify. These disruptions and distortions might need to be traced further back in time and/or further up the organisation. It is also helpful to keep in mind that every system is part of a larger system and as such, there may be a need to include the wider societal dimension as per the client example, below. This will certainly be the case if your team are at the helm of the organisation.

Angela had a crisis on her hands. She headed up the supply chain of a highly successful and rapidly growing global food business. Most of their geographies were tracking the growth acceleration curve, except for their US business. In this case, there seemed to be a continuous cycle of issues that blocked the flow of the product.

Each time she thought she had gotten to the bottom of the operational issue, another problem popped up further up or down the value chain. Customer orders were not being fulfilled and their reputation was being severely impacted. In addition, the US Region had been identified as one of the countries with the highest growth potential, and the global budgets (and reward mechanisms) had been established on this basis. The personal impact was being felt far beyond the US and her own reputation was starting to come into question. The impact of the gap in performance was so significant, they brought in external consultants to help, and a few strategic initiatives were deployed with some success, but this was not enough. There seemed to be a never-ending series of breakdowns each time they thought they had solved the problem.

When the additional layer of systemic inquiry was incorporated, it became clear that Angela was dealing with several disruptions in the ordering forces, dating back to the formation of the organisation in the US location. We will come back to these in Chapter 7.

It is also worth keeping in mind the butterfly metaphor mentioned in Chapter 1, whereby each of us has two interconnected butterfly wings on our backs. The primary, larger of these wings is influenced by the family system and the other, smaller wing, is shaped by the organisational experiences encountered.

You might uncover a dynamic mix of organisational and personal patterns that have become intertwined. The good news is that the collapse of these two contexts can be highlighted and explicitly separated again so that all parties can become more consciously aware of this tendency.

In addition to the overlay of organisational and personal systems, you sometimes find that patterns attract patterns.

For example, if a member of the team is a child that ended up looking after a sick parent and therefore assuming the role of grandparent for the rest of the family, there is a strong likelihood that they've learned to step up and absorb responsibilities far beyond their remit. This act will have taken place from a place of love and an intention to help and support and often, at a cost to themselves.

This formative history will pre-dispose them to doing something similar in the work context. At some level, these dynamics are familiar to the individual and that familiarity breeds comfort.

Patterns attract patterns

Put simply, systemic patterns in the organisation can attract individuals with similar patterns in their personal system. This individual may be unconsciously attracted to roles where there is something missing in terms of what is required from a strategic leadership dimension – they unconsciously discern that their need to be of significant help has an opportunity to be satisfied. It will probably feel like a perfect match for them. However, this pattern of stepping up into the space may not necessarily serve the rest of the team.

In fact, it is more likely to weaken the team and significantly impact the relationship with their line manager, and the person stepping up could, in fact, be 'cast out'. Their well-intentioned act of stepping into the void may be perceived as arrogant and taking too much space which will negatively impact the level of trust and the sense of being a 'line of one'.

How Limiting Patterns Form

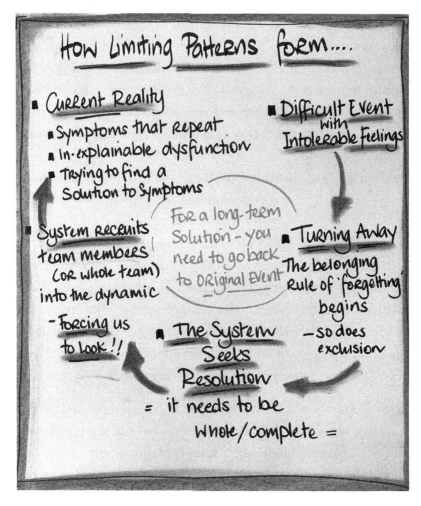

Limiting patterns form when something difficult happens. As a way of surviving and staying in the system, i.e., maintaining their fundamental sense of belonging, people look away from the difficult incident because it is too confronting.

As an example, if someone significant is exited from the business under a veil of secrecy or silence, everyone knows what has happened but has silently agreed to look away. This event becomes a part of the history that is too difficult to talk about and so, it metaphorically slips into the shadows. It is simply too painful to look at the reality of what has happened at that point in time. And so, the belonging rule of not talking about it, of looking away, starts in that system. And so, the exclusion begins.

When we agree to look away, for the sake of our belonging, exclusion begins.

As mentioned in Chapter 1, the survival mechanism of the collective is to be complete. In this endeavour, the system will find a way of remembering the parts or experiences that were excluded. In this search for completeness, dynamics will continue to surface through a variety of routes. These dynamics can show up through an individual or at a functional level and may not be a positive experience for either party!

Regardless of how it is showing up, it will keep repeating until it gets the attention that is required. The wider system will sacrifice the individual for the sake of the whole. With this approach, you can intervene such that the individual does not have to be sacrificed and before the relationship is destroyed.

How to Facilitate Movement

From a systemic perspective, movement is enabled through precise language and the utilisation of physical space. This combination of sentence work and the utilisation of space is arranged into specific interventions that are designed to access and address specific patterns and root causes.

When we refer to space, this can be literal space if you have your team in a face-to-face setting, but it can also be a virtual space. These precise sentences are designed to fully expose the root cause, acknowledge their impact, and dis-entangle those elements that have been disrupted over time.

The precision and sequence of the sentences are important as they are designed to connect with the less conscious part of the system and those that are unconsciously representing the parts of the system that need attention. You need to get to the heart of the issue and connect with the primary pain points. As always, tone and pace are critical.

The Overarching Process

There are three broad steps to unlocking the system so that it can move towards its highest potential – described in the visual below:

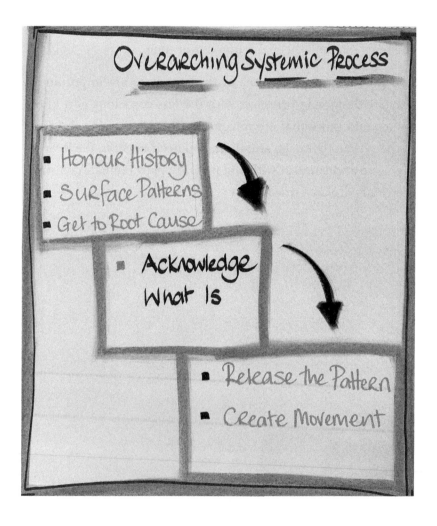

If you are working 1:1, this process can take place in one extended session. When you are working with your team, it can still unfold within one session, however, be careful not to prioritise speed over quality and depth. Consider when it might be more appropriate to slow down and work at the pace and depth the team is ready for.

Don't assume that just because you are ready to dive in, the team is too. Consider whether you have fertile soil and if not, how you could create the psychological safety and conditions for the team to feel comfortable to delve 'beneath the floorboards'. We'll pick up on creating psychological safety in more detail, in chapter 4.

Practical Application

Let's shift from the principles to the application. The 3 x H model overleaf, is a way of moving through the systemic process and positioning the work to be done. When enough space is dedicated for depth of inquiry, exploration, reflection and co-creation, this process can enable the movement as an aligned, united, and healthy team, mentioned above.

It is recommended that you schedule these key stages over a series of sessions rather than trying to cram them into one event.

You can read more about the application of the 3 x H Process in several of the client case studies and within the resources section, in chapter 12.

Some percolations:

Percolations are intended to support your reflections as a leader. I encourage you to spend a few minutes capturing your thoughts and ideas that emerge. If it feels right, these musings might be worth bringing to one of your team development sessions as a platform for a rich conversation.

- When issues arise, how quickly do you jump to the obvious conclusion?

  ○ How can you create a new discipline where you pause, zoom back, and explore more deeply?
  ○ Who can support you with embedding this leadership practice?

- How can you honour history within your team?

- How safe do your team truly feel in bringing issues to the table?

  ○ Think about the last time one of your team members raised a concern:
  - How did you react?
  - What space did you provide for this to be fully understood?

  ○ What could you put in place to create a safer environment?

- What repeating patterns do you notice within your team?

  ○ Which of these is serving the team?
  ○ What might be limiting and what is the impact?

- Are there particular roles in your team where you notice a repeating pattern, regardless of who is in the seat?

° When did this start?

° What was happening within the team and/or the wider organisation around the time this pattern started?

PART 2

THE TEAM IS FORMING – BUILDING HEALTHY FOUNDATIONS

4

CREATING THE CONDITIONS FOR PSYCHOLOGICAL SAFETY AND BELONGING

There has been a lot of material published over the last few years around the importance of psychological safety and as such, this topic deserves a chapter in itself.

An environment where we can bring our full, authentic self
Feel safe enough to not know
AND
To challenge without fear.

When we reference psychological safety, let's assume we are referring to a culture where team members feel safe enough to:

- Be vulnerable
- Bring their full and authentic selves
- Be OK with not having all the answers
- Ask for help
- Challenge the status quo without fear of retribution.

As the leader, you have a huge impact on the tone that is set and the extent to which psychological safety is established in your team. As per the research shared in the opening chapters, leaders impact the climate by circa 50-70%. This influences the levels of discretionary effort volunteered and ultimately correlates with the bottom-line results by circa 28%.

A critical component of success as a new leader is the ability to bring the existing team with you as you'll hear more about in the client example that follows.

When leaders are asked to shift their line of sight to the wider and longer-term horizon, they are being asked to take a different position in the team. This elevated view of the future is a necessary responsibility of leadership but if you are not careful, it can be experienced as a position of 'power over' by the rest of the team and when that happens, social connection can be lost.

Power over as a leadership position can unconsciously trigger an amygdala reaction in others and have them withdraw to an inner sanctum for safety. This will be especially heightened for those that have experienced a strong power over dynamic in their own personal history.

You can read more about how you can maintain or regain this human connection with your team in Chapter 10, Time to Look Inwards.

Taking the Team with You on the Journey

———

Shivaun had been a member of the team for some time. Her promotion to the CEO seat was significant. On one hand, being appointed into her first global CEO role was what she had been working towards for her entire career and on the other, she knew it was going to be a significant challenge. She wasn't convinced that she was the right person. There was competition for the role, and she was going to be stepping into her boss' shoes. He was being moved up to the next level in the wider organisation and was still going to be her line manager. From an organisational standpoint, she was the right choice. She had already worked in various parts of the organisation and understood how things worked, she had the respect of her peers, and she was dedicated to the vision, mission, and purpose.

Nevertheless, she was asking herself if she would have rather been given an opportunity to run a business and team that she didn't know. She was wondering if it might have been a bit easier and less complicated if she was starting from a 'clean slate' and didn't' feel beholden to her predecessor's ways of running the business and the team. From a systemic perspective, at least, clean slates rarely exist. There's always some history that has got us to where we are today – even for founders.

The context meant that her boss would not change – the reporting line would remain, and her new team had previously been her peers. Her style was very different to that of her predecessor, and she needed to find a way to make this role her own. She wanted to establish a new place from which she could lead the team and the business into the next chapter.

She could have felt her hands were tied but, she embraced the opportunity for a 'respectful reset'. Shivaun fully embraced the systemic approach and had external support to facilitate a healthy endings process with her line manager to ensure the CEO seat was clean and fully available (more information on this in Chapter 5).

In addition, as a team they took the opportunity to map the history (with her predecessor in the session) and to celebrate his tenure in the role (more on this in Chapter 8), thereby clearly drawing a line between one chapter and the next.

Shivaun needed to establish a sense of psychological safety so that the team felt comfortable enough to identify and agree on new ways of working that did not feel disloyal to their previous leader. Most of the team had been appointed by her predecessor – it was a delicate balance.

After the celebration of the history, she involved her team in mapping each of their places in the team, relative to the team purpose, so she could position how she wanted to lead. She also invited them to share what they needed from her (more on this in Chapter 6).

By working through this complexity carefully and with the 3 x H framework in mind, Shivaun was able to galvanise the energy in the team and together, they hit the reset button.

Prioritise the Team Development Agenda

Going slow now will enable you to go faster later.

In addition to being self-aware and intentional, it is recommended that you prioritise dedicated time and space for the development of the team. In the same way that you would not expect a new customer to invest in your premium-priced products or services without building a platform of rapport and trust, you cannot expect team members to put themselves 'out there', without a similar investment.

The significance of this is further emphasised when we bear in mind that the ultimate survival mechanism at an individual dimension, as mentioned in Chapter 1, is that of the need to belong. Your team will be able to withstand a significant amount of disruption and ambiguity, and stand 'shoulder to shoulder' including during restructures IF they have a deep sense of belonging. When you manage to establish this, the team will feel accountable and be at stake for each other. It is a huge asset and a source of resilience in the toughest of times.

Make this investment up front and you will reap the rewards later. Consider how you can create opportunities for the team to get to know each other beyond their job role and beyond the task at hand. As mentioned in Chapter 1, each person brings their family system and their limiting patterns with them, consciously or otherwise. It's helpful for colleagues to understand each other's journey so far, including their potential triggers and their patterns. Sharing this as early in the process of forming helps to build and accelerate trust.

This increased understanding can be enabled through a dedicated space in each team meeting or perhaps a series of dedicated team development sessions. To build this into the DNA of the team, it is recommended to incorporate a mix of both, especially in your first twelve months as a forming team. You will find some examples of frameworks you can utilise to support these sessions in the resources section in Chapter 12.

Create a Shared Context

When teams have a consistent and shared understanding of where they have come from, they can more easily and quickly align on where they are going. This is even more important when there are new members joining the team partway through the journey.

As referenced in Chapter 3, the 3 x H framework really helps to bring the systemic approach into practical application. The first part of the framework (Honour History) involves mapping out the history to include the founder of the team, founding principles, key milestones/events and all the key people that contributed to the team that exists today. You can access an example and a full list of what needs to be included in the resources section in Chapter 12.

This detailed mapping of all the chapters of the team and 'the contributors' that made it so, ensures the team are in respectful listening mode in the first instance. It creates a moment to zoom back and acknowledge the entirety of what it has taken to get to the current state. This also helps to mitigate the propensity to move into solving mode too quickly. This is not helpful and will probably mean that you are dealing with quick fixes to surface-level symptoms. In addition, it will only trigger unconscious resistance to the ideas offered as they are likely to be experienced as being disrespectful to what or whoever has gone before.

Take some time to recap the history and, to highlight the patterns that seem to be repeating. This can help to de-personalise what is happening in the team and the wider organisation as experienced in the client example below.

———

Archie took over the CEO role of a family-owned business in the transport sector. The organisation was primarily driven by two members of the family, who were not on good terms with each other. They had decided that they would step back from the day-to-day running of the business and agreed to appoint a CEO role. On 'face value', the business was going well – they were leveraging the societal shift towards more eco-friendly forms of transport. They had a strong brand; a good reputation and a significant part of the growth agenda was geared towards driving international expansion. They needed a CEO with global experience.

Archie had been appointed for his expertise as a CEO and, for his experience in the internationalisation of brands across the global landscape. His experience from an adjacent sector was directly transferable. The family were keen to bring in fresh thinking and to develop the existing executive team, most of which had been in place for a considerable period.

Within six months of his arrival, Archie realised he had a challenge on his hands but couldn't quite put his finger on what it was or where it was coming from. He'd already done his due diligence on business performance, established key metrics and reviewed the customer base. He had clarified the vision, got the team on board with it and had signed it off by the family members. As far as he was concerned, they were good to crack on.

However, this was not proving to be the reality. There seemed to be a lag factor. Despite an agreed vision and priority to drive internationalisation, there was a series of divergent activities dedicated to maintaining business as usual in the current regions in the background. There were scarce resources, and they were being diverted and diluted without his knowledge. To top it off, relations with the family members felt strained.

Archie was really starting to question himself and his decision to get on board.

As part of the team development agenda, Archie decided to bring the executive team together. In addition to dedicating time for a meaningful check-in (more info on this later in this chapter), the team were invited to get involved in mapping the history (as part of the 3 x H framework).

Through this mapping process, they were encouraged to zoom back and review how the business had been built up to the current context. As part of that, they were asked to identify any limiting patterns that seemed to repeat over the years. Through this process of exploration, they were able to make sense of the churn of the CEO role. There had been three predecessors before Archie.

With the distance created by zooming back and looking at the longer time horizon, Archie and the team could de-personalise the situation and see that this divergence of strategy was not new and was not wholly theirs to own. It became clear that the split in the family was showing up in the organisation via two separate streams of activity that were competing for scarce resources. Archie's predecessors had also found themselves in a no-win situation, trying to mediate between the estranged family members. The churning CEO role was the symptom that kept repeating.

This process really helped to create an understanding of

the shared context. The team were more alert to the fact that they were being unconsciously pulled into the dynamic of bypassing the CEO and driving both strategies out of loyalty to the family. As a team, it became clear that there was a critical conversation for Archie to have with the family.

They realised this was very little to do with Archie and everything to do with the systemic dynamics of working in a family system. They could empathise and contract with Archie in how they could ensure they stayed alert to these dynamics in the interim. It gave Archie a genuine opportunity to speak his truth and role model his humility and vulnerability.

This set the stage for the next phase of the 3 x H process - Being Honest about Reality.

Things You Can Incorporate Straight Away

A Quality Check-in Process

When you are gathering your team together, allow space for a meaningful check-in process. It can be tempting to rush through the check-in as a bit of a 'tick box exercise' but it's worth remembering, each of us is holding an implicit question of our new colleagues, as we embark on a journey.

**The implicit question everyone is asking of each other:
Can I trust you?**

When you bear this in mind, proactively building in space for colleagues to share a bit more with each other is where the safe container of getting to know each other is established.

Invite the team to share how they are, as well as what they are working on. Within a dedicated team development session, it is recommended that you encourage a more holistic check-in conversation i.e., to share from what's going on for them inside and outside of work. If it's the first team development session, and especially if the team don't know each other, it can be powerful to invite each team member to share a highlight from their personal history – see examples of frames you can utilise in the resources section, Chapter 12.

If this is unfamiliar territory, the team can benefit from someone role-modelling the process. It is highly recommended that the leader goes first to role model an increased depth of sharing, demonstrating appropriate vulnerability, humility, and openness. This creates robust foundations for psychological safety.

For a shift in behaviour - leaders must go first.

To support those team members that are more reflective, it is recommended that you send a few questions to frame the check-in process in advance of your gathering. Displaying these in the room before you kick off the meeting will also ensure that the more spontaneous members of the team have the frame to follow in the moment.

You can find some suggestions for a quality check-in process in the resources section, Chapter 12.

Percolations:

Percolations are intended to support your reflections as a leader. I encourage you to spend a few minutes capturing your thoughts and ideas that emerge. If it feels right, these musings might be worth bringing to one of your team development sessions as a platform for a rich conversation.

- If your team were to describe the current environment, what words would they use?

- How would the team rate their sense of safety:

  - To speak up
  - To acknowledge they don't know
  - To ask for help
  - To challenge each other

- To what extent do the team have a secure sense of belonging?

- When was the last time the team openly challenged each other?

  o How did you/they respond?
  o How can you create an environment where this happens more often?

- To what degree, do you have a shared understanding of the current context as a team?

  o What could you put in place to develop this further?

- How well do the team know each other?

  o How would you rate the level of trust in the team?

- How often do you dedicate time and space for genuine team development?

  o What could you put in place that moves the dial on this?

- Who can help you keep these essential ingredients on your radar?

5

HEALTHY ENDINGS ARE A PREREQUISITE FOR ROBUST BEGINNINGS

There is a Lot to Learn from Our Family Rituals

We are often better at handling endings in our families than we are within the organisational setting. Within our families, we are generally better at acknowledging the passing of a loved one – the ending of a life. In my own Irish family roots, we have our loved one resting in the family home in the few days between the 'passing' and the funeral. The extended family gather to pay their respects which in turn, creates the opportunity and space for a different kind of dialogue to unfold.

Stories are told, fond memories are brought to the front of the mind, and the essence of the person who has been lost is honoured and fully acknowledged for who they were. This helps to ensure the individual has their rightful place within the rich tapestry of the family history. This tradition creates space and support for the release of emotions, for the tears to flow and for the pain and loss to be acknowledged.

Although I didn't fully appreciate the importance of these family rituals in my formative years, I've come to learn how crucial they are. They provide a safe platform for those 'left behind' to be able to face the pain, accept the reality of the loss and say their goodbyes with the support of the extended family. This is an essential 'stepping-stone' for those remaining behind to be able to face the future. A helpful quote from one of the pioneers and an established author in the field of grief work, Elizabeth Kubler-Ross, comes to mind:

 "You cannot say hello until you say goodbye."

How Do We Handle Endings in Organisations?

Within the organisational context, we can often fall into the trap of taking a much more functional approach to endings and lose sight of the human dimension. We can neglect to provide support and space for the team/s to absorb, reflect, face the reality of the situation, and confront the break in belonging.

Some of the classic examples of when support for a healthy endings process is key:

- Major redundancies or de-layering, where close friendships and groups have had a strong bond and a sense of belonging.
- Unannounced departures of senior leadership, especially if this has been under difficult circumstances.
- Acquisitions, whereby the leader of the acquired business is released as part of the 'deal'.

- A change in the name of the organisation or a brand
  with whom individuals have established their sense of
  belonging.

This regression to functionality is especially evident when new
leaders can inadvertently trailblaze their way through their first
ninety days with the intention of creating a compelling case for
change. They unconsciously send a message of disregard (or
perhaps even disrespect) of all that which has (and those that
have) gone before.

This can immediately create an unconscious and increased
loyalty to the predecessor and ultimately create unnecessary
resistance within the team to the strategic plan moving
forwards.

An additional aspect that is often neglected is that when
individuals leave organisations, especially if they have been
there for a long time, they can leave parts of themselves behind
without realising it.

Their heart, soul and passion have been poured into the
business and the team for a considerable period. If this energetic
release is not attended to, part of them can remain in their seat.

It not only restricts their ability to truly move on, but it also
creates a challenge for the incoming leader and unconsciously
restricts the team from fully engaging in the new leader's vision
for the team. It is not necessarily visible but at an energetic level,
the team will be stuck.

Healthy Endings Process

This intervention is designed to clarify where systemic ownership lies, i.e., between the individual leaving and those remaining. It invites the outgoing individual (or team of individuals) to identify what they have contributed to as part of their role and that needs to stay with the organisation. The new systemic owner will have the autonomy to pick this up and build upon it as they see fit.

They are also invited to identify what they need to take with them for their onward journey. This tends to be parts of themselves – their passion, their heart, and their soul. These are crucial parts of themselves that need to be reclaimed.

This leaving behind, taking back, separation, and the explicit acknowledgement of each, is at the heart of this intervention. It is an immensely liberating but also an emotional intervention that needs care, time, space, and an appropriate environment.

In this context, we refer once again to the client example of Shivaun who picked up the CEO role from her previous boss.

We introduced Shivaun in the previous chapter – she was taking up the role of CEO of an established and incredibly successful global business. She was promoted from within the team and was stepping into her line manager's shoes. He was being moved up a level in the organisation, so he was still going to be her boss and an integral part of the organisation.

This could have meant that Shivaun would feel restricted to carry forward all the 'established' strategies and ways of working. She could, very easily, have felt stifled in her role.

Instead, Shivaun had the endings process facilitated between herself and her line manager. They witnessed and supported each other going through the process, starting with her line manager. He needed to leave and separate out what he would be involved in, to create a genuine space for Shivaun to step in. Circa 80% of the role was explicitly handed over to Shivaun and only 20% of strategic initiatives would be co-owned as part of the development work in the wider organisation. In the same way that her line manager was leaving his role, Shivaun was also leaving her previous role to her successor. In this instance, there were several endings being facilitated concurrently.

As we mentioned in Chapter 3, systemic language needs to be precise as we are working with the unconscious layers of the human psyche. There is a specific sentence that is at the heart of this endings process, which is designed to clarify systemic ownership:

"I created/generated/built xxx as part of my role. I did it out of my duty/love/care/passion...and I leave it with you to decide how you build upon this. I have no further claim to it."

To have several levels move up through an organisation simultaneously is very unusual and, in this instance, getting expert guidance and systemic facilitation support made absolute sense.

The net result is that Shivaun feels like she has the appropriate level of freedom and autonomy to drive the business into the next chapter and she has created space for her successor to also step up.

Shivaun has just completed her first year in the role, with her leadership team fully on board, they have met their performance targets, transformed their ways of working to be much more efficient and driven empowerment through the next layers of the organisation.

Preparing the Ground for Your New Starters

Having clarified systemic ownership and energetically cleared the 'seat', let's turn our attention to ensuring the existing team can welcome the new starter so that they can bring their full selves, including all their experience, to the role.

New starters bring a collection of experiences and skills as well as their patterns as mentioned before. A classic challenge for any new starter is to get the balance right between being respectful of who and what has gone before and bringing in fresh thinking. This is, of course, part of the rationale behind their appointment.

This requires spending an appropriate amount of time listening to fully understand the territory and not bulldozing their way into the role whilst, at the same time, feeling able to offer their ideas, expertise, and experience.

Most organisations put in place some element of an onboarding process for new starters, however, in my experience, the more senior the role, the less structured this tends to be. Senior leaders are expected to organise quite a bit of this for themselves. This leaves quite a lot to chance and doesn't necessarily set them or the wider team up for successful integration.

As a minimum, it is recommended that you put in place a transition period, within which, the new entrant is set up on a 'listening tour', and after this period, they are asked to share their insights, reflections, and recommendations on how things could be even better. The recommended transition period is a minimum of sixty and an optimum of ninety days.

You can further support a smooth integration by actively incorporating a systemic housewarming at the conclusion of this transition period. This involves creating an opportunity for the existing team to share the narrative of the journey so far and the context behind the ways of working and to declare the areas where they are open to ideas and wisdom from the new starter. The 'sacred cows' are explicitly declared, as is the appetite and space for innovation.

The brief for the new starter is to share what they carry in their 'rucksack', i.e., to share the headlines of their experience (both organisational and personal), including key milestones and their biggest challenges and moments of learning. From this place of humility, they are invited to share their observations and where they can see opportunities and bring their wisdom from other organisations.

If you haven't already included the sharing of personal contexts, personality profiles and preferred ways of working across the team, this is a perfect opportunity to incorporate this human dimension.

You can pick up more details on the application of the systemic housewarming process in the resources section, Chapter 12.

6

PURPOSE PROVIDES ORIENTATION
PURPOSE GALVANISES ENERGY

There's a lot of content available around the importance of purpose how it creates a clear point of reference for the team and a unique identity in the market.

Purpose sits beyond the strategic initiatives and the day-to-day operations. It galvanises energy and creates a narrative that employees and customers alike can align behind. Purpose is becoming even more important as society is increasingly conscious of and alert to the agenda of organisations and the degree to which they are operating from a place of mutuality.

An implicit question that most organisations need to be able to answer is how they are making a worthwhile contribution to society. This is especially true in the context of the sustainability agenda. No longer is it acceptable to pay 'lip service' to this concept of mutual exchange.

Purpose Provides Orientation and Fosters Belonging

Purpose exists at the organisational level and the team level. Ideally, there is a clear 'golden thread' that runs between the two. The systemic function of purpose is to provide a sense of orientation and to enable each team member to find their place, relative to their colleagues, in service of this purpose.

Purpose clarifies the reason for the existence of a team and what it is uniquely theirs to deliver. You can flip this on its head and ask yourself the question:

What would not happen if this team didn't exist?
If the answer doesn't flow spontaneously, you might have some work to do!

The aspect of finding one's place, relative to the team purpose, is often the source of hidden tensions. Some members of the team might be operating from the 'wrong' place whilst a few might be taking up too much space, thereby minimising the opportunity for others to fully occupy their roles.

The important thing to keep in mind from a systemic perspective is to de-personalise these phenomena. Stay curious as to what this is suggesting about the wider system and the roles the individuals inhabit, rather than the people themselves.

Ask yourself:

- What might not yet be clear regarding how the team roles fit/operate together?
- Have we distilled the roles that are enabling the others?

- When did these dynamics start?
- Where else, in the wider system, are you noticing the same phenomena?
- Of the dynamics that you witness, what might be rooted in the wider system?

You can read more about the root causes of tension about this critical sense of place in Chapter 7.

As mentioned in Chapter 1, the survival mechanism operating at the individual dimension is that of belonging and, as such, individuals will often need to make sacrifices (consciously and otherwise) to belong.

When we choose to belong to one team, it may feel at odds in terms of our belonging to other teams, especially if they feel like they have competing or conflicting agendas. For example, if you have a senior leadership team within a division of the business, each of your team members is not only part of your divisional team, but they are also often reporting into a central functional team in the wider organisation. The only variance is where they have 'dotted line' reporting versus 'full line reporting'.

Creating an environment where they can belong to both without feeling disloyal to either can be challenging. It's a delicate balance and it requires leadership that can operate in service of the business.

One of the ways you can proactively confront this dynamic is to keep the attention on the 'golden thread' of purpose, constantly encourage the team to zoom out, check alignment and remind yourselves that you are one part of the wider ecosystem. This requires a downshift in ego and an ability to hold a wider lens with humility.

Don't Force It - Let It Emerge

One of the biggest challenges, now that purpose is becoming an essential ingredient and to some extent, a 'badge' that leaders feel they must declare, is the tendency to feel compelled to 'nail it' quickly.

When we take into consideration the concept that the upcoming future is coming towards us regardless of our intentions and that part of the role of leadership is to stay attuned to evolving customer needs, then perhaps clarity of the purpose might emerge rather than be forced through a purely cognitive process. An example of this emergent approach is described in the example below.

Anneke was promoted into the role of President of a highly successful, large-scale global organisation. She had been a member of the team for circa five years and knew her peers quite well. As we know, moving from peer to boss can be a difficult transition at any level of the organisation. In addition, she was inheriting a big agenda from her predecessor who was going to remain in the business at the next level of leadership.

Her new team, some of whom had previously been peers, were exceptional leaders in their own right and most had deep expertise in the sector. Anneke made some clear choices on her leadership approach. She would leverage the expertise within the team, and she wanted the work on the purpose, vision, strategy, and five-year plan to be a co-creative process that was allowed to emerge from within the exploration undertaken by the team, rather than being driven from the 'top'.

As part of the lead into defining their purpose, Anneke fully embraced the systemic approach and first took time to honour the history of the organisation as set out in the 3x H process mentioned in Chapter 3.

They mapped all the key events, milestones, brand launches, acquisitions, and divestments, as well as identifying all the key people that contributed to the story so far, including those that exited due to difficult circumstances. They zoomed back to also include the mistakes, pain points, the breakthrough moments and ultimately, harvested the key learnings on the roadmap thus far.

Within the same session, they also took some time to honour and include each other's history at a personal level – they unpacked a few of the surface layers and started to lay down the foundations for authentic connection. It was still embryonic in terms of building the foundations for trust, but it sent a signal of the importance placed on the human dimension from the outset.

Next on their route map was to look at the wider landscape, to identify strategic risks and opportunities, including the ever-evolving needs of their customers and consumers, alongside the impact of technological developments. They started to crystalise where they wanted to place their energy as an organisation over the forthcoming five years. They took into consideration, how they could leverage their scale and unique position in the market and, importantly, how they could mobilise and align the wider organisation.

With this distilled, but not yet final, version in mind, they zoomed back again and asked themselves:
If this is the scale of the opportunity and what the market is ready for, what is our unique role (our purpose as an Executive Leadership Team) in relation to this business?
Who are we for the system and what is ours to do?
What are we uniquely placed to do that would not happen if we didn't exist?

What ways of working will energise, equip, and enable us to bring this purpose to life?
Sadly, the experience of working with purpose cited by many teams is one of hours and, potentially, days of mind-numbing 'wordsmithing' and a purely rational and cognitive level process. It feels so laboured that by the time they have finished, they have lost the will to live, and the very mention of their espoused purpose creates an allergic reaction.

Another familiar version is the obligatory race through the process so that the necessary box can be ticked and reported back to satisfy higher levels of management. Neither of these versions serve anyone in the value chain. Anneke's team distilled a first draft of their purpose and ways of working (including the behaviours) within one hour! It was a moment to acknowledge all the previous work that had enabled this level of clarity and the purpose emerged from all the mapping, insights, conversations, and reflections. It surfaced through the process, rather than being forced or created.

The team felt energised and congruent because they were able to draw the 'golden thread' between the wider organisational mission and purpose, their unique reason for being and how this could mobilise the rest of the organisation behind one plan. Every word (and there weren't many) meant something. It was a breakthrough moment.

Let's not assume that once the purpose is distilled, the work is complete. When we take into consideration the importance of remaining open and the reality that the upcoming future is constantly moving towards us, it is a good discipline to regularly sense-check your purpose, particularly when you have new team members coming on board.

Percolations:

Percolations are intended to support your reflections as a leader. I encourage you to spend a few minutes capturing your thoughts and ideas that emerge. If it feels right, these musings might be worth bringing to one of your team development sessions as a platform for a rich conversation.

- What's the 'golden thread' of purpose that runs throughout the organisation?

- To what extent is your team aware of this 'golden thread' between your organisational purpose and that of your team?

- If your team were asked about the team purpose, would they be able to cite it and describe it, consistently?

- If your team didn't exist, what would not get done?

- How would you rate the sense of belonging that is enabled by your team purpose?

- To what degree can each of your team members find a clear, available, and secure sense of place, about how they contribute to the team purpose?

- If you have inherited the team purpose from your predecessor, how could you bring a heightened sense of external awareness and openness to the process of reviewing your team purpose?

PART 3

THE STORMING PHASE

ITS ALL KICKING OFF

7

SYSTEMIC ROOT CAUSES OF TEAM DYNAMICS

The Systemic Patterns That Show Up in Teams

Let's remind ourselves why you need to illuminate the systemic pattern and get to the root cause. If you don't, you will be chasing a perpetual flow of dysfunctional dynamics and performance will be impacted. It will feel like you are treading treacle and you will be repeatedly challenging yourself if the effort is worth it. Get to the source of the issue and you will be able to stop the blood flow to the dysfunction and free the team up to get on with their work.

There are a variety of limiting patterns that show up in teams and we can generally trace them back to either a distortion or disruption of the ordering principles (time, exchange, place and belonging) or a tension between one of the three levels of conscience – both of which were referenced in Chapter 1.

This disruption could be taking place in the current context, or it may have taken place further back in time. If it is to do with something historical, the collective conscience, in its endeavour to bring the system back to completeness, will keep stirring things up until such time as attention has been garnered, root causes confronted, and the narrative is updated.

In the same way that trauma is carried through the personal system for up to three generations, as evidenced through research in the field of epigenetics, more recently, we are discovering this is also the case with organisational memory. Any unprocessed and unacknowledged trauma that has happened in the organisation will be carried forward and show up in lots of different places within the organisation.

This includes sacrificing certain individuals or functions and utilising them as messengers on behalf of the system. This will continue happening until the source event is fully seen, acknowledged, and remembered as part of the history, as mentioned above. Once complete, the nervous system of the organisation can stop holding on to the void and settle as you can see in the client example below.

I was facilitating a team session for a major FMCG organisation, producing household brands. They noticed that there was a problem securing the right candidate for the role of Asia Pacific President. As this was a key region of growth, this was becoming a critical business issue for the global organisation.

They had turned over three people in this leadership role within 12 months despite the best recruitment process and securing exceptionally strong talent. The leavers fed back to the business that they felt they couldn't stay – always a warning signal to take note of.

When the situation was unpacked from a systemic perspective, the root cause became obvious very quickly. The original setup of the region included two senior leadership roles, each responsible for 50% of the region. As part of a restructure, a decision was made to reduce the leadership role to one. This happened quickly and without due process or appropriate communication with the individuals involved.

The ordering principle of mutuality between the organisation and the exited employee was sacrificed for the sake of speed. There was no explicit acknowledgement of the lack of process, the contribution of the exiting individual to the business, or the consequent impact of this change on them or their team.

In fact, in the interests of speed and getting the region merged quickly, those remaining in the newly merged region were not proactively engaged in the process either.
There was no malice or negative intentions in this scenario, it was simply a judgment call by the leaders at the time, that prioritised speed above proactive communication and explicit acknowledgement. The remaining leader who was allocated the role of the newly combined region decided to leave after a few months –

they could not stay because of an unconscious level of guilt.

It would be very easy to assume the fault was with the leader or that their team were not accepting them as part of the organisation. The reality was that the role of the leader was burdened, and it was turning over good candidates ever since. As this region was of strategic importance, a member of the executive leadership team decided to intervene to ensure this issue was fully understood and resolved.

An inquiry was set up to explore what might be happening from a systemic perspective. We stepped back in time to get to the source event. The dynamic was showing up through the churn of this regional president role, but the source of the issue was further back in time. The systemic function of this limiting pattern was to bring the root cause to the surface. The collective system (and those within it), needed an explicit acknowledgement of the lack of process, the deficit of mutual exchange and its impact, to enable the system (and the team) to settle.

The current employees of the Asia Pacific region would not have been rationally aware of this need. Their need to surface the root cause was sitting in the unconscious but nevertheless, making itself known. This combination of zooming back, working at the right level and with the right individuals (those who were responsible for the overall system), meant that we were able to unburden the

Asia Pacific President role, settle the team and ultimately create the conditions for the team to realise the growth potential that had been identified.

———

Through the client examples that follow, the patterns will start to become more obvious, and you will have an appreciation of how tangible and significant the impacts are within a team.

The patterns detailed are not an exhaustive list but include those that you are most likely to come into contact within a team context. Often, you will come to realise that there is an intricate combination of systemic patterns driving the dynamics within a team. This work is not about working in straight lines. It is complex, sensitive and can be emotive just as is the case with human beings. Expect to uncover multiple layers. Be patient and get comfortable with some necessary detours.

It is important to bear in mind that some patterns may be rooted in the personal system of individual team members and that some of what may be happening is where patterns in the organisation are triggering the unconscious patterns within the individual.

The client examples that are included in this chapter describe the classic symptoms of each pattern and how they might manifest in a team setting.

Context Overlay

As this is one of the most prevalent patterns that you will encounter, recognising the symptoms and understanding the dynamics is probably one of the most important to have in your awareness.

This pattern is about two contexts being unconsciously collapsed together without the individual or the team, consciously realising it. This becomes possible when a previous incident or event has not yet been fully processed and integrated.

There are a few ways in which this can happen. It might be about two separate layers of the organisational context being collapsed together. For example, when a restructure communication is being shared, the experience of a previous traumatic restructure scenario (not yet fully processed and acknowledged) floods the conversation and is being projected on top of the current context. The unexpressed emotions are activated and 'on the table', which can be challenging and sensitive to navigate. This will be especially challenging to navigate without being disrespectful if the previous scenario was beyond your remit as a leader and the current team context.

Context overlay can also involve the personal context being collapsed and projected in front of an organisational scenario. For example, if an individual, as a child, experienced challenging family dynamics during a divorce that they haven't yet processed, they may find it hard to navigate the tension and dynamics associated with mergers and acquisitions when different parts of the organisation are being separated and brought together in different 'homes. This will be especially relevant and provoking for them if they are operating in a 'central role'.

The signals to look out for when this pattern of context overlay might be activated is a level of emotional charge that is significantly higher than that which is warranted by the current context as you'll see in the client example below.

The development opportunity in this scenario is to help the individual and the team, to separate the two contexts and realise that they are, indeed, different. The good news is that you don't need to be pulled into the content of the personal context in the team setting. It might, however, be appropriate to recommend individual support for the appropriate team member/s via systemic coaching with a qualified professional.

"Am I really that difficult to work with? The team move away from me rather than come towards me. They want to do their own thing and seem to find sanctuary in the silos of their separate business areas. Team meetings are transactional, and we are going through the motions. The barriers are getting higher, not lower, as I try to build the collective spirit. Everyone seems to be hyper-protective of their respective areas and resources. This is not the kind of leadership I recognise in myself or the kind of leadership team this business needs right now". This was the puzzle that Michael was trying to understand.

Michael was relatively new to the organisation but had a long tenure of experience as a senior leader behind him.

He was used to leading teams from diverse functions and nationalities and was very strong in terms of his intellectual horsepower. He could identify, shape, and define strategic challenges with ease and translate them in a way that most colleagues could comprehend. He was easy to relate to and could connect with people at all levels of the organisation. At face value, he had all the attributes for success as he entered this new role and organisation.

He had joined a highly successful, large-scale organisation that had a commanding position in its sector. He was given responsibility for a divisional leadership team, made up of a group of highly experienced leaders, each of whom had been in the organisation for a minimum of five years.

Despite this wealth of knowledge and expertise, Michael found himself unable to leverage these assets. Instead, he found himself witnessing a team that seemed to be cynical, inward focussed and competitive with each other. They were incredibly 'nice' to each other and polite with him, but they were highly suspicious of hierarchy, especially so with communication that came from the global headquarters.

With an intention to get to the bottom of this irrational behaviour, Michael took the team offsite, and they spent some time mapping their history, as outlined in the recommended 3 x H Model, referenced in Chapter 3, and illustrated in the Resources section.

They unpacked key decision points, key milestones, highs, lows, launches, divestments, breakdowns, and breakthroughs. Also included were all the people that had made a significant contribution to the team over the years since its formation.

Within a relatively short time, it became clear that there were some very difficult experiences trapped in the memory banks – unacknowledged and, yet, unprocessed. The level of emotion in the room was palpable. There had been significant restructuring introduced, directed by the global headquarters, and driven by Michael's predecessor. These changes effectively downgraded the place of the entire division (and the divisional leadership team) within the overall organisation.

The whole unit felt like it had been demoted and despite its performance providing a lion's share of the overall revenue, its sense of place was confused, and the scale of its contribution was unacknowledged.

When working with a systemic perspective, it's important to remain curious about the total picture, to remain judgement free and to seek out the facts of what happened and why. Remember to separate the roles from the people and finally, and most importantly, it is critical to directly acknowledge the truth and scale of the impact.

Michael had inherited a situation whereby the team interpreted any communication or initiative that came through his role as untrustworthy and a potential threat. His team did not feel safe in his presence and so they protected themselves by retreating into their functional silos. The previous experiences with his predecessor were unconsciously attributed to Michael's position as a context overlay.

In addition to the context overlay, the unit did not have a secure sense of place in the business and Michael needed to consider how he could ensure the unit was appropriately acknowledged for its continued contribution to the wider system, without it seeming like they were the 'spoilt children' who were demanding attention.

This was not a straightforward leadership assignment!

Exclusion

Exclusion is about omitting a key piece of, or a key contributor to, the history from the current narrative. The system's survival mechanism is constantly scanning for and seeking to be complete. In this drive for completeness, it will continually trigger and surface patterns and dynamics that force the current incumbents to look – to review what is going on and to remember what has been forgotten or avoided.

This can often take the form of dysfunctional dynamics, that in reality have little and sometimes nothing to do with the individuals or team through whom, these are manifesting.

This exclusion can happen at an individual, team, function, organisational or even a societal level. As a society, we are becoming much more alert to the societal dimension and our collective responsibility in this regard as evidenced in the client example below.

———

Let's bring our attention back to Angela and her supply chain challenges, introduced in Chapter 3. You may recall she was appointed to lead the supply chain of a large-scale, global business and although overall growth was phenomenal, she had a crisis on her hands in the US organisation. There was a constant succession of operational challenges that were significantly impacting global performance ratings.

The external consultants helped them to identify operational glitches and realised that their systems and processes were not designed to cope with the accelerated levels of growth in the timescales required. Transformation of the entire architecture was underway, but there was limited, or at least very slow, progress. It would have been very easy to assume the core issue was Angela and/or the capability of her US Team. After some exasperating months of continued supply chain breakdowns, and with support from the global leadership team, Angela sought external expertise to bring a systemic lens to the situation.

Upon further exploration and by unpacking the history of the formation of the US business set-up, Angela realised she was dealing with something much more profound than an operational challenge in the supply chain.

As they reviewed the US locations and the scale of the land acquired to set up the manufacturing sites, they came to realise how much had been taken away from the indigenous people of the local communities. Their heritage, and the land that would have been deemed as sacred land, was consumed by industry - this had not been acknowledged. This critical milestone in the US history line of the organisation had been excluded.

This was not just the case for Angela's organisation, it was attributable to industry more generally in these locations. Nevertheless, the balance of give and take was not healthy.

Angela, together with her colleagues, sought to address this exclusion and the imbalance in mutual exchange. First and foremost, they included and fully acknowledged the impact of the historical events in their updated narrative and made several generous and symbolic donations to the indigenous communities. It was a significant moment of genuine and heartfelt giving and receiving.

Six months later, the newly architected systems and processes were starting to bear fruit and the year-on-year stats spoke for themselves.

Angela delighted in sharing: "We have experienced amazing transformation – there is a very different energy on-site, and we have significantly moved the dial on most of our key metrics".

These included moving the dial on quality by six percentage points, improving the service to customers from 35% to 88% and reducing staff turnover from 40% to 4%.

As you may imagine, none of these interventions are quick fixes – they require the investment of time, energy, and attention. You need to get the team off the operational agenda and look wider and deeper. This investment will pay off tenfold in the medium and longer term.

Identification

When there is exclusion, one of the ways in which the system brings this to our attention is by recruiting an individual, team or function (hereafter referred to as 'the element') into the vacuum.

The recruited element will not realise it, but they are sucked into the space of representing that which has been excluded and will often manifest the characteristics of the excluded part.

**When a key element of the history is excluded,
The system will find a way of pulling something or someone into the void.**

The element that is pulled into this void is a symptom bearer, in the same way, that within a family system, unresolved issues within the parents will show up as symptoms in the children.

For example, if there has been a significant restructure that has been executed with speed and without the opportunity or the space for careful communication and a healthy endings process, it is very likely that another part of the business, e.g., the function that had to absorb the resulting overflow of workload, may not be able to operate at its optimum, yet will not understand why at a logical level. It has become identified with the exited employees.

Classic symptoms of this pattern include the identified part experiencing feelings or displaying the behaviours of the excluded part so that they are not forgotten. This may manifest as the identified element wanting to follow those that have been exited.

At some level, they feel guilty for the loss experienced by their previous colleagues and a way of staying connected with them is to energetically (and unconsciously) 'check out 'of the day-to-day operations.

Another classic sign of identification is a sense of fixation, whereby the identified element is compelled to look at that which management can't. Through this fixation, they are drawing attention to that which needs to be confronted and remembered. This will only become obvious when you attend to listening in a more holistic and embodied way, as described in chapter 1.

Another example of how this dynamic shows up is when an individual is exited without exploring the real drivers of the presenting issues, and without an appropriate and respectful ending. The lack of exploration and trying to avoid the truth of the covert exit will often result in the successor portraying the exact same behaviours and tendencies that got their predecessor fired!

It is very easy to assume that it was just bad luck to have two bad recruits, or that the identified individual or team is the core issue, however, once the truth is exposed and the exclusion of the real issue is acknowledged, the identified people are released from holding the dynamic on behalf of the system.

The time horizons may vary. This pattern of identification can also be relevant in the current context. It might be that a member of the team is identified with a part of the organisation that has been excluded or, for some reason, does not have a voice at the table. This spokesperson can be interpreted as a rebel, the 'black sheep' or perhaps even the troublemaker. In these instances, stay curious and delve deeper.

Keep asking yourself: What might this problem be a solution for?

When we ask ourselves this thought-provoking question, we might get to the intention behind the uncomfortable truth-telling.

Identification often happens within the organisational context. It is not unusual, however, to also observe the personal context being unintentionally brought into the organisational setting as you'll discover in the client example below.

Geraldine had recently been appointed to her first Leadership Team role. Her colleagues welcomed her with open arms since she had already been working in the organisation for some time. She was taking responsibility for one of the largest divisions in terms of revenue generation. It was the backbone of the business but in the past eighteen months, all the key metrics were showing a slowing of organic growth, a downturn in performance and a worrying loss in market share. There was a lot to do but her boss had confidence in Geraldine - she knew the sector and the team intimately.

But Geraldine was concerned. Despite her background knowledge and expertise, she was struggling to find her place in the leadership team. She felt like she couldn't quite pull herself away from the periphery. Each time her business area was in the spotlight, she deferred to her colleagues for their input, rather than declaring her perspective and would subsequently get frustrated with herself as she knew she was uniquely placed and super clear on her viewpoint. This sensation was not exclusive to the work setting – she also found herself confronted with similar frustrations in her personal life. This holding back was identified as the limiting pattern she needed to resolve.

At face value, it looked like she was having a confidence crisis and the 'water cooler whisperings' were suggesting that perhaps she had been promoted too early or, worse still, maybe she had already reached her natural 'ceiling' in the previous role. Thankfully, her line manager wasn't convinced by the noise and put systemic coaching in place as part of her twelve-month development plan.

Through systemic exploration, the layers were peeled back, and it was discovered that Geraldine was identified with her maternal grandmother. Based on her heritage and the family dynamic at the time, Geraldine's grandmother could not take her place in her family of origin. She was always kept at the edge, occasionally invited in, but never really felt safe to do so. She kept herself on the periphery of the family circle and constantly felt separate and excluded. She could not find a secure and safe sense of place from which to contribute to the family.

The behavioural dynamics witnessed in Geraldine were remarkably like the grandmother she was clearly identified with. This was Geraldine's unconscious way of staying in connection and the family system's way of keeping the grandmother included.

From a systemic perspective, Geraldine was operating out of 'blind loyalty' to her grandmother, and by adopting her behavioural patterns i.e., staying on the periphery of things and not taking centre stage, Geraldine was not taking her full place within the leadership team. She was playing small.

When this could be exposed for what it was, without judgement, and Geraldine could fully acknowledge her grandmother in a much more conscious and healthy manner, she was ready to be released from this identification dynamic.

Releasing someone from holding these dynamics is not like a 'light switch' but it does happen relatively quickly and typically creates a huge sense of relief and release for the individual. They feel like a burden has been lifted and they have the possibility to move in a way that they couldn't before. This is the case whether it's identification at an individual or collective level.

In Geraldine's case, within nine months she went on to become one of the strongest and most resilient members of the leadership team and won a global award for her masterful turnaround of the division. This intervention provided breakthroughs for the business and for Geraldine in her leadership and her life beyond work.

This is a great example of the patience and intentionality that are needed to get underneath the complexity of team dynamics. With care, consideration and deeper exploration, exponential results are possible for every part of the system.

Distortions of Place

This is a prevalent pattern in organisations and creates a lot of tension within teams – most of which will remain unspoken and fester underground.

The order of time has a close relationship with this pattern, as mentioned earlier. Sometimes it is necessary to make explicit the various hierarchies of time within the team – this can help to cut through the noise and settle the nervous systems particularly when there is some jostling for place. This explicit acknowledgement is another manifestation of honouring history.

For example, it may be helpful to make more explicit who has been in the team the longest and who came later. It might also be important to clarify who is the most credentialed/experienced for the task at hand versus who might be in the earlier stages of competence building. And bearing in mind this is not an exhaustive list of examples, another layer may be the length of experience in a particular discipline e.g., organisational leadership role versus the earlier stages of functional leadership.

This clarification is especially relevant in the formative (or reforming) stages of the team and enables the team to really see and acknowledge each other. It is a relatively easy and very practical way in which you can apply the methodology of 'acknowledging what is'.

When something is missing at a certain level, e.g., leadership, the system will seek to find something or someone to fill the void. The void may recruit certain roles, but it might also recruit an entire function.

This pattern is as relevant in the organisational system as it is in the family setting. If this pattern is active in your own personal family system, then you are more likely to be predisposed i.e., an easier candidate to recruit. It is vital to emphasise that none of this is happening at a conscious level and there are consequences, both positive and limiting.

Whilst there are some inherent gifts that can be harvested from stepping up that are likely to include increased exposure and lots of learning, this distortion of place is not a sustainable way of operating in the longer term. It involves carrying more responsibility and over time, this will feel burdensome, and the individual may, in time, experience burnout, feel resentful and potentially be estranged from their peers.

This distortion of place can often be seen during times of restructuring, where a key aspect of the change management process has been neglected and a particular function or person steps into the void with the best of intentions. If this is for a temporary period and is explicitly acknowledged, there isn't an issue. Most people can accept that there's an important task that needs to be done.

As mentioned earlier, distortions of place can happen at the individual level, but it is also possible for an entire function or division to be sucked into the void as the system's way of forcing attention on what is missing.

This can happen to any function, but one of the teams that tends to both display the patterns in the wider system and get recruited into a void is the HR Team. This function has various names in different sectors and organisations. In this context, we refer to HR regarding the guidance, facilitation and support required around culture, leadership, talent, learning and all aspects of providing great working conditions for employees.

As their systemic function is to help leaders create the conditions for exceptional performance through people, their boundaries are naturally more permeable than some of the other functions. Because of this, the HR Team is fertile soil for being utilised by the system to surface that which cannot be seen.

An entire function can be recruited as the symptom bearer of the wider system.

What happens within the function may not just be about HR, but perhaps a pattern that the whole organisation needs to address.

In addition, because HR is typically connected to all areas of the business and employees, they are more likely to pick up the essence of what is vibrating in the system and be the 'truth-tellers'. This reinforces the need to have strong business partnering in place with your HR function.

If YOU are leading the HR function, be mindful of the weight the team may be carrying – it might be that YOUR TEAM IS NOT THE ISSUE. Take time to unpack the layers and discern what is theirs and where your function (or individuals within it) may have been utilised as symptom bearers.

A valuable intervention that might help diffuse some of the tension is to first de-personalise and normalise the phenomenon, acknowledge the void and honour the intention of helping.

There are two main variations of being pulled into the void, as follows:

Triangulation

Put simply, the family equivalent of this dynamic is when a child is recruited to fill the void left by one of the parents. This is typical in a single parent family or if one member of partnership is not fully available. This could be due to extended periods away from the family, sickness, or addiction.

Within the organisational context, an example of triangulation happens when a direct report is pulled up to the same level as their line manager. This will happen when someone or something is missing at the manager level. The manager is potentially seeking a sounding board and unconsciously pulls someone 'up' alongside them for discussion, sharing and ideation.

As mentioned earlier, if this is a temporary scenario or the pulling up is universally happening with all members of the team, as required, this is not necessarily a distortion of place that will incur the consequences mentioned in the introduction, above.

Whilst this pattern is taking place between two individuals within the team, there is a significant impact on the team dynamic if this is an ongoing phenomenon.

For the manager, it is potentially because something they need is missing and on the part of the triangulated individual, they act out of a desire to help. As you will note in the example below, the key issue arises when the manager is divulging important information that is not shared with the wider team and puts the direct report in an elevated position in terms of knowledge. This can be an incredibly uncomfortable position for the direct report. For those that are vulnerable to it, it can also inflate the ego. Whilst it is an unconscious manoeuvre, in the long term it is not healthy for either party.

It is, however, important to acknowledge the gifts of being triangulated. These include, but are not limited to, honing the ability to quickly attune to others and from that increased sensitivity, anticipate others' needs. 'Others' in this context would include more senior stakeholders and clients.

However, the triangulated individual can end up feeling exhausted by trying to fill the gap whilst also doing their own role, and potentially feeling like they are not quite in either position fully, i.e., they are neither a peer nor a direct report.

This can create tension, jealousy, and confusion in the team dynamic and, in time, tension in the relationship between the line manager and the inflated direct report. Unless the individual can find their way back and settle into their 'actual role', they may find themselves exposed and at risk of being spat out of the system.

Let's come back to Issac, the newly appointed UK CEO, introduced in Chapter 2.

Issac gave himself some time to understand what he had inherited and the scale of the challenge in front of him. He knuckled down, set aside quality time to get to know the business and established, quickly, that he needed a coherent strategy that was attuned to the long-term view of the sector and in particular, an acceleration of the digitalisation agenda.

He was new to the business but not the sector, so he needed help in acclimatising to the nuances of the organisation. He sought out a few experienced members of the team to lean upon as part of his onboarding.

These relationships helped him get off to a great start. They provided him with a font of historical knowledge and context, which enabled him to be on the 'front foot' in terms of how to get his key business topics onto the leadership agenda.

Issac needed to establish a new vision, strategy, and plan with the team and to bring them together as a coherent leadership team with an enterprise mindset, rather than a group of individuals predominately preoccupied with their functional/local agendas.

As part of this process, he continued to incorporate one of his confidantes within the team, Simon, in his thinking as he added a lot of provocation and value to the process. Together, they were able to develop the thinking to the next stage and then bring it to team to develop further and finalise.

On the surface, this seemed to work well. Issac would talk through the first draft thinking and open the discussion up with the team. It would become very clear, very quickly, however, that Simon had been integral to the early thinking. In the first instance, there was a bit of awkwardness for Simon, but it didn't seem to affect the quality of the final output.

This formula of utilising Simon as his first sounding board became part of their weekly meeting rhythm. It was becoming obvious to the rest of the team that Issac was more reliant on Simon, and they were starting to feel excluded. Tension was building but no one was overtly talking about it.

Moreover, Simon was being put in an elevated position with more information than the rest of the team, including downloads from Isaac's Executive Board meetings that were not appropriate to share. Simon was unconsciously recruited into a triangulated relationship. He had been pulled up to operate as a confidante and sparring partner for Issac.

Whilst this was a valuable resource and outlet for Issac, it was having an impact on team dynamics. Simon was becoming disconnected from the rest of the team. It was impacting his fundamental sense of belonging and it was starting to cause a split in the team.

It is possible to address a distortion of place if the core issue is surfaced and acknowledged. Once this happens, the team will settle, and the triangulated individual can re-establish a social connection and belonging in the team.

We'll cover the interventions to address all distortions of place in the resources section of Chapter 12.

Parentification

Parentification is the phenomenon of an individual being pulled into the vacuum ABOVE their line manager. The parallel in the family system would be the child stepping up to look after a sick parent, and therefore taking the place of the grandparent.

If someone is or has been, parentified in their family system, they are a prime candidate for being recruited into this pattern in other settings. As is the case with each of these patterns, this is not a conscious choice and is enacted out of a positive intention to help carry the load.

When senior leadership is missing, individuals (and sometimes whole functions), with the very best of intentions, are recruited into the vacuum and end up in the inflated position of managing their manager. It might be exhilarating on one level, but it is a precarious position for anyone to find themselves in.

Some functions may be closer to the CEO for example and before they know it, are playing a bigger role than is appropriate for the organisation. This has a huge impact on team dynamics and yet again, the invitation is to zoom out and stay curious as to how this has evolved.

In the short-term performance might be maintained but this issue can create corrosive dynamics in the wider team in the longer term. AS the book title suggests, in this scenario, the team is NOT the issue. There is a vacuum of leadership in the wider organisation.

The signal you might notice in the parentified team (or individual) is one of perceived arrogance. They seem to occupy a large space and within themselves, feel more equipped to deal with situations than those roles that are designed to do so.

In terms of body language, this might even be visible. One of the classic traits is the chin being held high, which may make it seem they are looking down their nose at others. This can come across as disrespectful and is likely to estrange them from their peers and potentially create a split in the team.

In addition, classic characteristics include finding it difficult to accept authority from others and they are likely to feel above senior management in terms of capability. It can be a lonely place to inhabit.

Nevertheless, it is important to acknowledge there are some gifts to be harvested from carrying this additional load associated with parentification. They tend to be very resilient. They have a strong degree of self-reliance and are resourceful.

Because they readily and often proactively, take on more responsibility, they may find themselves climbing the career ladder quickly and/or gaining exposure. However, they may also regularly find themselves and ostracized and on the edge of burnout. It's a big price to pay as evidenced in the example below.

"I'm the only one who sorts things out around here – you can't rely on anyone else. How can they let me go at a time when I'm the only one in this team who knows how to do this properly?" was the frustration and confusion expressed by Ryan.

Ryan found himself exited from his organisation and didn't really understand why. He was a senior HR professional with decades of experience behind him. He had worked in various locations around the globe and for the first time in his career, he found himself on the other side of the exit conversation. He did not see this coming!

He'd had a new boss appointed several months earlier. As far as Ryan was concerned, she was not ready or qualified for the job. As a business, they were mid-way through some major transformation, which included restructuring at least 50% of the workforce.

Picking up the responsibility for the various change initiatives before they collapsed was a familiar pattern for Ryan. From what he could see, his manager was hiding behind the fact that she was still in her onboarding phase and was already leaning heavily on him to pick up the slack. As for the rest of the team, they were not competent enough.

Ryan was confused and deeply frustrated. He had never been in the position of being out of a job before and felt that he had been taken for granted. How could they possibly execute this phase of work, without him? With some encouragement and an outplacement package to support his transition, he decided to take some time to delve deeper and understand how he had ended up here.

He unpacked his career history on a timeline (as outlined in the resources section of Chapter 12) and realised that his pattern of taking over, grabbing responsibility for the critical tasks in major projects and viewing most others as incompetent had been running for some time. This has an increasingly negative impact on the team atmosphere. He seemed to be at the centre of most of the strategic projects and had kept himself very separate. He stayed at the edge, never really feeling like he fitted in with his peers or with his boss. He wasn't sure where his loyalties were and didn't really feel like he belonged in any one community. He was, however, aware that he felt much more comfortable in meetings with senior stakeholders when he was helping them scope out the next phase of whichever project was next on the list.

The history mapping process shifted to his personal trajectory, and it became evident very quickly that Ryan was parentified in his family system.

He was the eldest of two children of divorced parents and was pulled into the role of mediator and an emotional crutch for his mother from a very young age. At an unconscious level, he was pulled up into the inflated role of parenting his mother, who took the divorce badly, and of looking out for his younger sibling. He stepped up 'two levels' in the family system. He learned not to rely on those that should have been looking out for him. In addition, he had to learn how to take control and be totally self-sufficient. He developed an accentuated bias for independence.

With this trajectory, Ryan was a prime candidate for being recruited into any vacuum left by the absence of leadership within the organisational setting. Given the urgency and the scale of the transformation agenda in the business, he acted with good intentions, deep care, and a desire to help. Over time, Ryan took on the unconscious belief that they, i.e., everyone else, were incapable of doing things properly and he would just take control, to the point where everyone stood back and let him get on with it.

This pattern of taking the bigger place had translated into the organisation as arrogance and disrespect. He was not perceived as a team player or a collaborator. Consequently, when the function itself was being restructured, he was a prime candidate for an exit package, despite being one of the most experienced and expert members of the team.

Upon reflection, Ryan realised that he could have been more attuned to the consequences of being the solo player. The organisation, on the other hand, also had a responsibility for proactively managing a void of expertise, if this was indeed, the case.

For the individual who has been parentified, they need to be more alert to their vulnerability of being sucked up into the void and, if it's necessary, ensure they can find their way back to 'stand' alongside their peers. One of the attributes that can help with getting back into social engagement is humility, the essence of which is about having a perspective of the bigger context and being the right size within it.

In summary, when you zoom back, there is a responsibility for senior management to ensure that the right level of capabilities is anchored in the team for the context of the business and the task at hand.

In the absence of this, individuals will be pulled up into the void and they may have to face the positive and negative consequences of being willing to take on the extra responsibility.

Polarisation

Let's think about this from a personal dimension to start with. When we are polarised, we inhabit a part of ourselves and disown the other part. There is a split. There's a part that we feel comfortable with. We find the other dimension repulsive and tend to feel better than it. The reality, however, is that both parts exist within us. We embody this 'other part' without realising it.

We embody both extremes of the polarity without realising it

The area that has been most explored regarding this systemic pattern is the polarity of victim and perpetrator. What we know is that each victim also embodies the essence of the perpetrator, i.e., their behaviour. Some aspect of their life embodies perpetrator energy. The same is true the other way around. This duality is outside of conscious awareness.

The pattern of polarisation is calling attention to the fact that both parts want to come together and reconcile a split that has happened further back in time. This spit can show up within the team and most often, has nothing to do with the team members themselves. The separate parts of the team can, however, seem deeply entrenched and it can feel almost impossible to reconcile these two parts.

The crux of the matter is that at some point in time, or further up the organisation, a split has taken place and because it hasn't been fully acknowledged at the time or at the right level, the split is playing out elsewhere in the organisation as you'll see in the client example below.

The good news is that once you can acknowledge the causal event and bring a larger context to the landscape where the two parts can co-exist, integration is possible, and the team can move beyond the polarity. This enables the team to be freed up from the dynamic of feeling pulled and repulsed by the other and harmony can gradually return.

Let's come back to Issac, the newly appointed CEO for the UK element of a family-owned business, referenced above.

As alluded to earlier, Issac had a challenging role and a clear brief to turn the UK business around.
As he set about this challenge, he kept noticing the repeating pattern of a split. It was showing up in lots of different ways, including with the leadership team.

Despite having launched a clear vision and strategy and set a host of strategic initiatives underway, the bottom line was that the team still weren't pulling together as a cohesive whole. They were operating as a group of capable and experienced individuals who saw their own teams as their 'first priority'.

Dysfunctional dynamics, which included covertly undermining each other and following their own agenda in isolation, continued to play out behind the scenes. This was particularly the case between certain team members. It would have been very easy to put this down to personality clashes, which did have some validity.

However, this was beyond and deeper than that - there was an overall sense of a split in the team.
In one of the first team development sessions thereafter, the honouring history intervention was incorporated,

and the team were invited to map the history of the organisation.

This process is a very visual, and physical timeline of the history, which includes all the key events, milestones, launches, divestments, M&A, restructures, and the highs and lows. It also includes key contributors at each stage of the journey. It is a process that helps to embody the critical systemic component of inclusion. At certain points, the team moved into sub-teams so that they could continue to contribute to the history pieces they were aware of and could bring them back to the overall storyboard.

When the history map and story were complete, the team were invited to zoom back and view the overall timeline.
As mentioned earlier, this family-owned business had previously acquired one of its key competitors and employees from both companies were in the leadership team.

It became obvious that the acquisition of the competitor and its impact on both companies, at the time, had not been fully acknowledged.
The identity of the acquired business had been lost and with that, their sense of belonging. The host business had not been acknowledged for its fortitude and quiet and industrious wisdom. The cultures of the two businesses were distinctly different.

It is fair to say, that each of the businesses, on an energetic dimension, were 'running in parallel' for some time, rather than as an integrated whole. They had not really come together.

This is where the split originated. When this could be seen and fully digested, the team could appreciate the pain experienced in the other 'side' of the acquisition process. They each made the effort to understand how that experience was and a more respectful level of empathy ensued.

The intervention that interrupts this pattern of polarisation and helps the team to grow beyond it, starts with zooming back. This enables the team to comprehend when/where the split happened and to see a larger context within which both dimensions can, and do, exist.

To grow beyond the polarity, you need to help all parties to see the broader perspective within which it doesn't have to be an 'either or'. There is a broader context within which each polar opposite, in fact, needs the other to be complete.

This pattern of polarisation can also show up in the organisation, as workers vs management or region vs headquarters. As we know, each of these elements is needed to make a stronger, whole organisation.

In addition, some of the classic situations where this dynamic may be further triggered include restructures, redundancies, mergers, and acquisitions.

Summary

You will often find there is a complex combination of organisational and personal layers and competing levels of conscience that have become interwoven over various time horizons. There is usually more than one pattern or dimension that sits underneath the dynamics in your team.

If you don't get to the root cause you will find yourself on a perpetual cycle of quick fixes that deal with surface level symptoms that have no lasting impact and meanwhile, team performance suffers.

The systemic approach will help you unpack these layers and get to the root cause. When this is (or these are) surfaced and fully acknowledged, the next phase is to harvest the gifts and release the patterns so that the team and the wider organisation can move towards its highest potential.

This methodology is not about deploying quick fixes. It requires care, sensitivity, and an investment of time. Identifying the root cause and acknowledging the consequences thereof is where the main body of work needs to be done.

Once this acknowledgement has happened, the system and the team within it, already start to settle – there is more receptivity to the next and final phases of disentangling the team from holding the dynamics.

This in-depth and precise approach will enable you and your team to breakthrough the dysfunctional team dynamics and move the whole system towards the potential that you know exists.

The ideal timing to incorporate this approach is when you are forming your team so that everyone can fully understand the platform they are building upon. Whilst it is ideal to set off on your team journey with this approach established, it is not unusual that it's only when things get stormy and the tried and tested solutions aren't working that there is an appetite for something different.

Percolations

Percolations are intended to support your reflections as a leader. I encourage you to spend a few minutes capturing your thoughts and ideas that emerge. If it feels right, these musings might be worth bringing to one of your team development sessions as a platform for a rich conversation.

- What repeating symptoms/patterns do you notice in your team?

- Where are they showing up?

  ◦ What seems to trigger them to come to the surface?
  ◦ What's the impact of these patterns?

- When did this start?

- What might this pattern be a solution for?

- What might this pattern be trying to communicate on behalf of the system as a whole?

- What might have been disrupted (in the current context or historically)?

  - A sense of place?
  - Mutual Exchange?
  - A sense of belonging?
  - Has something (key event) or someone been excluded?
  - Vacuum of Leadership?

- What needs to be seen or acknowledged that up to now, wasn't possible?

- What might the evolutionary force of the future be provoking you to consider?

  o What might have reached its destiny, and is ready to come to an end?

8

HOW TO SURFACE AND MOVE BEYOND THE TENSION

It is helpful to keep reminding yourself that the overarching objective is to enable the system (and the team within it) to move towards its highest potential. To facilitate this movement, the starting point is to identify and acknowledge where things have become heavy or stuck.

When things get challenging with a team, it is very easy to assume it must be a clash in personalities, so you have the company-approved, psychometric profiling done on the team and, to be clear, this is a valuable thing to do and there is a place and time for this.

You set up various off sites to share these and to help the team to get to know each other better and whilst there are some natural clashes in terms of preferred ways of working, what you are experiencing seems to be beyond that.

Next stop – you decide to do a bit more work on the 'strategic plan' and priorities with the assumption that perhaps the tension might be about a lack of clarity on the vision and how each of the roles fit into that. Sadly, that familiar foreboding feeling comes back around quickly.

You can't quite put your finger on it, but you can feel the tension vibrating in the team, just under the surface. If this sounds familiar, then there's a good chance that you have more of a systemic issue on your hands.

The source of this tension might be related to a distortion or disruption of the systemic forces within the current business context but perhaps rooted beyond the team, i.e., further up the organisation. Alternatively, you may need to scan back in time to identify the root cause. Either way, the tension needs to be brought to the surface so you can work with it.

There can sometimes be a reluctance to go back in time and when this is the case, stay curious as to what might be driving this. This is information in itself. The reality is that looking back in time is often where you will find the root cause of the dynamic that is showing up in your team.

When you meet this resistance, it is helpful to remember that none of us can go back and change what has happened, but you can fundamentally shift the relationship that people have with past events and how they are held in the narrative.

The task entails surfacing the tension and being comfortable enough to have this in plain sight and creating the space for a deeper level of conversation. When the root cause and its consequences can be fully seen and acknowledged, you have already made a significant step. This might require some time to settle before introducing the appropriate intervention to release the limiting pattern and the associated dynamics.

There are choices in how to deal with this root cause, including specific interventions that range from pure conversational pieces and structured interventions to multi-dimensional mapping. The essence and objective of the key phases mentioned above remain the same.

This chapter does not set out to equip you to facilitate every possible systemic intervention. Rather, it is designed to expand your systemic lens, share the essence of the most helpful and appropriate interventions, and highlight the fundamental capabilities required.

There is no substitute for having a systemically trained professional alongside to support you and the team with this work but the content that follows will hopefully give you the confidence to confront the hidden tensions and take your team conversations much further than you may have done previously.

Key Principles

From a systemic perspective, movement is enabled through precise language and the utilisation of physical space. This combination of sentence work and the utilisation of space is arranged into specific interventions that are designed to address specific patterns and root causes.

When we talk about space, this can be literal space if you are working face to face, but also virtual space. The utilisation of space can really help to de-personalise issues. If you can imagine, the team are externalising an issue through the mapping process – this creates some literal distance, from which to view the issue and therefore also helps to reduce any defensiveness that might be triggered in a more conversational approach.

These precise sentences are designed to fully expose the root cause, acknowledge the impact, and dis-entangle those elements that have been disrupted over time.

As always, tone and pace are critical

Work Within the Remit of the Team

It is important to be careful to work within the remit of the team. Do not try to solve issues that belong elsewhere, e.g., to a higher layer of management or in the case of a family-owned business, be careful not to stray into working on the family dynamics. This will only parentify the team and make them too big and potentially unconsciously trigger an element of disrespect.

It is, however, entirely appropriate to zoom wide and understand the wider dynamics and context but be mindful of what is yours to address.

Managing the pace is key

One of the essential skills to master is pacing, alongside the confidence and courage to hold the tension. Don't rush over the painful, sensitive, or awkward moments – that's where the 'gold dust' often resides.

If the team are unaccustomed to this approach, or they are in the early stages of establishing psychological safety, it may take some time to reveal all the layers. It is important that these are seen and acknowledged before introducing an intervention. By slowing down, you also provide space and time for a diverse team to let the reality of what has been revealed sink in, in their own way.

Be careful to manage your own expectations on pace and not to immediately respond to requests from the team, to speed up. These requests will come in many forms, explicit and otherwise. However, they manifest, they are probably rooted in discomfort with the tension and/or acknowledging the truth of what is. It is in these moments, where you will need to depersonalise the resistance and courageously hold the tension, but with compassion.

Going slow to start with, as uncomfortable as that might be, will enable the team to go faster later. It takes time for these layers to be revealed and acknowledged. Only when this dimension is fully exposed and understood, should you move the team towards the appropriate intervention.

Know that this work doesn't have to happen in one team session. It can be spread across several meetings if they are in relatively quick succession to maintain the quality of the dialogue and the momentum as you will discover in several of the client case studies to follow.

Acknowledge the Original Pain Point

A helpful analogy in this context, might be to think about what happens when you have a significant injury. You initially ignore its severity. At a certain point in time, the pain becomes unbearable. You eventually acknowledge that you have been naïvely hoping that it will sort itself out with time.

In the meantime, your body has been compensating and secondary pain points have surfaced. A problem in your lower back has now progressed to a tightness of your neck that is stopping you from sleeping through the night and you have sharp pains in your knee. The strategy of painkillers and 'burying your head in the sand' clearly hasn't worked. There is a realisation and acceptance that you need to do something about it.

When you go to the doctor, their first instruction is to ditch the painkillers so that it is possible to locate the primary pain and distinguish it from the referred pain caused by your body trying to compensate.

Of course, the doctor will take into consideration that you need to ease the pain in your knee and your neck, but if the core issue of the back pain is not resolved, other pains will just keep showing up. Ditching the painkillers isn't always welcome advice or easy to do, but you realise it's necessary.

So is the case within the organisational context.

You need to pinpoint the primary pain and let it be really seen and fully understood. It's important to delve beneath the compensating layers and identify the original wound (the root cause). Working at this deeper level requires exquisite emotional intelligence and courage and the willingness to carve time out of the busy diary. You are likely to be facing a significant amount of resistance, particularly if this root cause is something that has been avoided for some time.

Once you've got an understanding of the underlying function of the pattern, i.e., what it is trying to do on behalf of the whole system, the root cause and its impact, the next stage of the process is to create movement via an appropriate intervention.

The Scale of Your Interventions

As mentioned earlier, you need to ensure you are working with the appropriate time horizon and context to affect long-lasting transformation. To carry through with the analogy of the human body, if the underlying cause is a faulty heart valve, the long-term and sustainable solution would be to undertake surgery to repair the valve.

From a systemic perspective, this is called a 'second order' intervention. We are working directly with the root cause and the source of the pain.

If, however, the patient wasn't ready for heart surgery or the prognosis suggested the operation would be too dangerous for them, then the doctor could prescribe medication to help regulate the rhythm of the heart alongside better nutrition to reduce fatty tissue around the valve. This combination of interventions would settle the symptoms and certainly provide some relief from the pain. From a systemic perspective, we call these 'first order' interventions. We are treating the symptoms and ultimately helping them feel more comfortable in the here and now.

If we follow this analogy through and take a wider scan of the environment, we might find longer-term solutions that have a sustainable impact over time. If it was becoming apparent, that there was a significant uplift in this specific medical condition in the local area, it would be worth exploring what had changed in the environment. This could include a lack of diversity in the quality of local produce.

The longer-term solution in this scenario could include a petition to the local council to get government funding for local farmers for increased diversity in their produce. This is more of a societal intervention, which has a longer and wide-ranging impact including for future generations. From a systemic perspective, this is called a 'third order' intervention.

In summary, 'first order' interventions will help settle the current system (and the team within it). An example of this is the intervention of 'line ups' that deal with the multiple complexities of place and hierarchies within time and within the current team, as mentioned in Chapter 2. However, if the root cause was more of a repeating pattern linked to an event further back in time, then the likelihood is that a 'second order' intervention is required so that you can resolve (or at least acknowledge) the source event and create the conditions for a more sustainable impact.

First order interventions are relatively straightforward to self-facilitate. You may, however, prefer to have a systemic practitioner alongside you for second and third order interventions with the team. Within chapter 12, you'll find resources that help get you started on the path of gradually integrating this approach as part of your leadership lens.

The Mindset Required

Bringing the right mindset to this work is vital, as highlighted in Chapter 1. In addition to the overarching mindset of 'problems are often solutions in disguise', it is also worth knowing that blocked life energy can show up in lots of ways. Frustration is one of the symptoms of this dynamic and if the frustration has nowhere to go, it can manifest in the relationship with the leader or the team facilitator.

It is important, therefore, to remember to depersonalise what is happening, in the knowledge that the current incumbents are often messengers and symptom bearers on behalf of the system as a whole. One of the patterns that is regularly in play within the system is that of context overlay, as described in the previous chapter. A classic signal of which is a level of emotion that is beyond the current context. This emphasises the need to establish some foundations of psychological safety, otherwise, the emotion will either go underground or find a safer place to vent.

This awareness and understanding will help you to stay free of judgement and maintain your curiosity. When the team don't feel judged or blamed, more systemic intelligence will reveal itself.

Critical Capabilities

There are a range of capabilities that will enable you to integrate the systemic approach as part of your leadership. There are three foundational dimensions to master.

1. Zoom Back and Wide

This is one of the biggest and most critical capabilities to develop. Learning to zoom back and wide, to look beyond the obvious, to stay curious and get to the source of issues is important when working in this way. This is as relevant for working with individuals as it is for teams. A key component of this is being able to manage the pace of the process and to pause before interpreting what is revealed.

When you can, invite the team to zoom back. It enables a wider perspective and, from there, you can identify the repeating patterns within the wider system and more fundamental dysfunction. There are often strong links between what is playing out within the team context and the wider organisational system. Don't assume these are always separate events.

This will ultimately help pinpoint the likely root causes, which is where you ideally want the team to lean in and to 'do the work'.

2. Listening Beyond the Noise

It takes time and practice to attune to the information being communicated by the system, rather than the literal messages in the here and now.

Start to build your capability to notice. Go beyond the cognitive, practical, and logical. Pay attention to your own embodied sense of what you are picking up. As mentioned earlier, our bodies are highly attuned sensing devices with more information running from the gut to the brain, rather than the other way around. If only we would pause on the over-processing, cognitive part of ourselves to listen to this instinct more often.

There is huge value in getting more comfortable with not knowing and acknowledging it. By declaring this, you can galvanise shared curiosity within your team and set off together on a discovery mission. Ultimately, the messages from the wider system, which is always seeking completeness, will make itself known.

Whilst you are listening, take a moment to check which system is communicating through this team member (or members). It might be that their personal system has been activated by the situation or they could be a symptom bearer on behalf of something in the wider context. Look wider and deeper - resist the urge to move into fixing mode too quickly.

As you will have picked up in the myriad of case studies, there is often a complex web of dynamics and systems in action simultaneously. This makes it even more vital to zoom back, listen on another level and dedicate time to carefully and respectfully unpack these layers so that a more sustainable solution can be identified.

When you attune yourself to the system, you can tap into a more precise quality of questions that will help you get to the heart of the matter.

Attune to the system- hone your skills to listen on another level.

3. Precision Questioning

The precision and sequence of the sentences in systemic work are critically important. They are designed to connect with the less conscious part of the system and individuals within it. The quality of the questions will impact how quickly and how precisely you can identify the core issues.

It takes an equal amount of courage and compassion to utilise this skill. You will need to master the precision of a surgeon, whilst embodying the care of a midwife. This will entail being comfortable enough to cut into the wound with clear, straight, and deep lines, whilst being prepared to follow necessary detours to protect or retrieve vitality.

When you have mastered de-personalising the presenting dynamics, you will be more comfortable and competent in naming truths without blame or judgement. This will, in turn, create a safe space for the team to also speak to theirs.

You will find a sample of core systemic questions that you can use at any stage of the systemic process, in the resources section of Chapter 12.

The Systemic Process

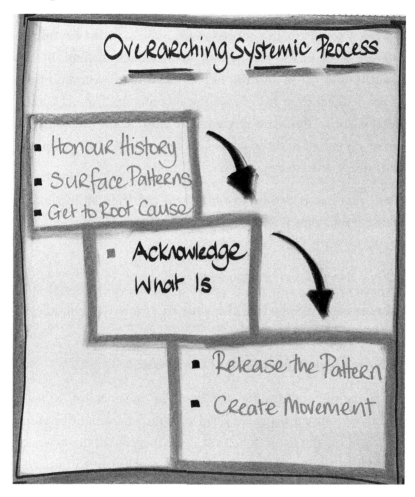

As the visual above demonstrates, here's a reminder of three key stages in the systemic process. Your challenge in the first instance is to surface the hidden dynamics and acknowledge their impact. This may be on specific individuals or roles but more often, they have an impact on the wider team and potentially, the wider business. If we stop there, we haven't moved the dial.

You need to get to the source event, which might be from a different layer of the business or further back in time. In any case, the root cause and the impact need to be seen and fully acknowledged, even if none of the incumbents from this time horizon are in the team anymore. You are acknowledging the impact on behalf of those who can't, and to serve the system as a whole in its drive to be complete.

When this has had time to settle, you can then shift gears to releasing the pattern and facilitating the energising movement.

Surface the Tension and Dynamics

There are several ways in which you can surface the dynamics in the team, which include:

Gathering Stakeholder feedback in advance

Incorporating stakeholder feedback in advance of a team session certainly gives you a head start on what might be going on in and for the team. It is unlikely to identify all the layers or the root cause, but it certainly creates a platform to initiate a meaningful conversation. You could use this to move onto a structured piece or a 3D diagnostic mapping – see the notes below.

The conversational approach is much more fluid and will require a robust platform of psychological safety within the team, such that they feel comfortable responding to the incisive questions offered.

You could move the team into break-out sessions to explore these questions together, which might make it feel a bit safer. You will find an example of this (Systemic Housewarming) in the resources section of Chapter 12.

Conversational (utilising precision questioning)

For the conversational approach to be most effective, you will need to hone your ability to attune to the system and be attentive to which layer of the system is responding, whilst also discerning if you are working with an organisational issue or a personal issue that is being unconsciously carried into the organisational context.

Structured interventions – providing some structure within which you be open to what emerges

If you are in the relatively early stages of incorporating this methodology, the structured approach is a good place to start.

The structure provides a container of safety and control for you and the team. This way of operating also creates context and clarity for everyone in the system whilst also providing space for the core issues to emerge.

There are specific structured pieces in the client case studies as helpful reference that bring this approach to life (history map and systemic housewarming). These are also included in the resources section of Chapter 12.

3D Diagnostic Mapping - Being open and responsive to what gets revealed

Finally, the 3D mapping process is a systemic facilitation process that needs to be held together. It has some structure in that you are mapping the key components of a system and clarifying where the boundaries are.

It is a highly interactive process and can provoke multiple layers to be revealed simultaneously through the mapping process itself. This approach relies on your ability to trust your instinct and embodied listening – knowing when to pause the team conversation and delve deeper.

When the first draft of the 'map' is complete, you can invite the team to zoom back and by precision questioning, another layer of insights can be revealed.

The overarching objective of this method is to create a 3D visual of all the layers. This can identify the patterns that are helpful, competing, dysfunctional and otherwise. By doing so, you will have a physical representation in front of the team which means there is no hiding place.

This approach can be quite confronting. It does, however, create a robust platform to move to the next stage of acknowledging all of what is and exploring the source. Examples of the 3D mapping process are incorporated within extracts of Isaac's and Shivaun's case studies.

Acknowledging What Is

This is one of the most critical steps in the systemic process. It is where you will probably experience the most tension, but it is also the element that offers the most healing. It is important not to hide away from speaking directly to the truth and spelling out the consequences of what has happened.

Do not underestimate the healing and settling power of the 'acknowledging what is' phase of the process. This is an intervention in itself. It creates the platform for you to hold the tension in your team and manage the pace before moving on.

Without this vital step, you are achieving only a temporary movement in the team dynamics. Once again, we pay attention to the specificity of the language, as well as its sequence within the acknowledgement phase. You can find examples of these in the resources section, Chapter 12.

When the full scale and impact of the issues are acknowledged, you are ready to shift gears to the appropriate intervention that will ultimately enable the movement.

Releasing the pattern

Before any limiting patterns are released, there is one final step. It is important to harvest the gifts that have been gained from carrying this pattern on behalf of the system. Without these gifts of learning, the team would not be where it is today.

Which Intervention?

In the current business environment of increasing pace and complexity, you won't be surprised to be reminded that there is likely to be an intricate mix of patterns that are simultaneously activated in your team dynamic.

This is especially the case if the team have recently experienced significant changes such as mergers, acquisitions, and restructuring. In these circumstances, confusion and/or distortion of the ordering principles happens regularly. These scenarios can also trigger unprocessed trauma sitting just under the surface. As mentioned earlier, unprocessed trauma will keep coming back up for attention until such time as it is fully acknowledged and integrated.

It is highly likely that more than one systemic intervention might be required to support the team moving towards their highest potential.

Bear in mind and be sensitive to the fact that the team also need to be ready for this approach. There is some care required to help them prepare and be aware of not trying to do too much too soon. Each of these interventions is untangling an unconscious way of operating and can be unsettling. New ways of being will need time to emerge, settle and be integrated.

Create Movement

Once the limiting pattern has been unravelled and revealed, and the impact fully acknowledged by all relevant parties, the system's need for completeness is met and the dynamic can settle. Having satisfied this endeavour to be complete, the team is primed for movement.

When we speak about movement in systemic terms, we refer to this as literal movement as well as metaphorical. Wherever possible, set up the environment so that the team can embody this act of stepping forwards as a whole-body experience rather than a purely rational one.

When the complex mix of dynamics is truly disentangled, the movement often happens naturally. There will be an energy that is released and the innate desire to move is fuelled by the upcoming future. You can stimulate this further by laying out the physical space in time horizons – clearly marking the direction of the past, present, and future horizon.

Summary

There's a lot in this chapter, so let's summarise the key themes:

- There are three key phases in the systemic process, starting with surfacing the tensions and dynamics; there are a few ways in which you can reveal the dynamics, and these vary in the degree of structure. It is recommended that you start with a more structured intervention if you are not familiar with the systemic approach.
- One of the most important dimensions, but one that is easily brushed over, is the middle step of acknowledging what is. This is where you create oxygen in the system, you give people permission to stop holding what doesn't belong to them and nervous systems settle.
- You will feel resourced if you can de-personalise all the dynamics and the noise; stay curious, suspend judgement, and keep asking: What might this problem be a solution for?
- Critical capabilities include zoom back so that you can attune to the wider system, listening at a deeper level and precision questioning.

- Trust your felt sense and embodied knowing – your body is a highly tuned sensing device.
- You might encounter resistance to look back – remember you cannot go back and change what has happened, but you can fundamentally shift the relationship that people have with past events and how they are held in the narrative of the team.
- There is no substitute for having a trained systemic professional alongside you, nevertheless, you can immediately develop a new way of scanning the team and there are some practical application pieces you can gradually build into your team development conversations.

Percolations

Percolations are intended to support your reflections as a leader. I encourage you to spend a few minutes capturing your thoughts and ideas that emerge. If it feels right, these musings might be worth bringing to one of your team development sessions as a platform for a rich conversation.

- Which of the critical capabilities might be the place for you to start building your systemic expertise?

- Given where you are with your team journey, what's the right moment to introduce this perspective?

- How could you prepare the team for this level of inquiry and dialogue?

- To look objectively at the patterns in your team, how wide and how far back in time do you need to zoom?

- Where are the boundaries in terms of what is appropriate for you to include in your map?

9

YOUR ROUTE MAP

The route map below, gives you a 'bird's eye view' of the recommended process of taking your team from stuck, to surfacing the dynamics and the tension, acknowledging their roots and ultimately, facilitating progressive movement. This route map incorporates the overarching systemic process outlined in the previous chapter and the practical application of this via the 3 x H model, as referenced in Chapter 3.

Bear in mind that you might not deploy all stages immediately or in the same session. It might be about unpacking the layers that are ready and then coming back to pick up the rest. Don't underestimate the value of giving the team space to reflect and digest. It's OK to be one step ahead but be mindful of not pushing so hard that you end up creating resistance.

PREPARATION

- Create psychological safety
- Healthy endings
- Systemic Housewarming – integrate new members.

HONOUR HISTORY

- Map the History

  º Include and acknowledge all of what (and who) has been before

BE HONEST ABOUT THE PRESENT

- Identify the patterns, the root cause, and the pain points.
- Surface the tension and acknowledge what is.
- Pattern release – harvest insights and learnings

CREATE HOPE FOR THE FUTURE

- Mapping the context – landscape scanning
- Let the team purpose emerge
- Agree a clear flow of leadership

  º Let everyone take their place (relative to the purpose)
  º Contract on mutual exchange between members
  º Clarify ways of working, including decision making

º Agree a rhythm & cadence of coming together that enables agility & flow

MAINTAIN MOMENTUM

- Revisit and refresh the purpose in context of the evolving market.
- Take time to reflect on what the team needs from YOU – not the other way around

PART 4

THINGS ARE STARTING TO SETTLE

DON'T GET COMPLACENT

10

TIME TO LOOK INWARDS
YOUR LEADERSHIP

Let's peel back the layers to the human dimension.

Science shows us that everything is made up of energy. Pay attention to your own energy – as a leader, it matters. Your energy has the potential to directly influence the levels of discretionary effort offered by the team and it directly correlates to the 'bottom line'.

Research tells us that the human heart rate can be picked up 1.2 metres (four feet) away by animals. Within nanoseconds, they can detect when there is a discrepancy between what your body is communicating and the words you are projecting.

The human body is a hyper-vigilant sensing device

The human nervous system is also highly intelligent. Extensive information is picked up via a constant, unconscious scan for safety. The vagus nerve is the longest nerve in the autonomic nervous system and runs from the face to the throat, chest, and belly. Approximately 80% of the information gathered through its fibres runs from the body and up to the brain, not the other way around.

You are constantly sending signals to other people's nervous systems

It is worth contemplating whether you are sending signals that suggest safety or if you might be triggering a fear response. When people are in fear, their capacity for social connection is significantly reduced and they are immobilised in terms of meaningful work. When people feel under threat, which is a natural response to change, they will mobilise for safety. The terms that are often utilised in this context are fight, flight, or freeze.

Our ability to regulate our nervous system is much less conscious and more directed by our bodies and informed by our formative years than we realise. We will have been significantly influenced by formative relationships and, with our primary caregiver. In these early years, we will have absorbed and inherited their patterns regarding how we respond to threat and our ability to reach out to others. To put this into context, of the 86 billion neurons in our brains, 10.75 billion of these have our primary caregivers in them. In most, but not all cases, this will be the mother.

A great quote to keep in mind, from Moshe Szyf, an expert in the field of epigenetics:

 "Our mother is in every cell of our prefrontal cortex."

Whilst these formative years clearly have a significant impact, neural development is within your gift and through ongoing self-development, you can deepen your awareness and expand your range of responses.

As a leader, you are expected to have a line of sight over the immediate horizon. You are ultimately responsible for scanning the environment and setting the team and the business up for longer-term success. This elevated position of horizon scanning and gathering a greater level of insight gives you a clear sense of responsibility, a meaningful contribution to the mission and boosts a sense of belonging.

However, this elevated position can also come across as a 'power over' style of leadership. When a leader shifts into this 'power over' mode, there is a break in the quality of social connection with the team. This can trigger an automatic sense of threat and have a negative effect on resonance with the team. A helpful definition of resonance is the ability to read one another.

Humility enables social connection to be maintained

One of the attributes that enables resonance and connection to be maintained, or at least retrieved, is humility. In this case, we refer to humility as keeping ourselves at the right size in relation to the bigger picture. When you can embody a humble approach and hold a dual intention for social connection AND driving the team mission, you have a chance of keeping the team with you on the journey.

Be alert to the state of your own nervous system and ensure you are resourcing yourself. The state of your own nervous system will influence and determine the quality of leadership you provide. You will find some hints and tips on this later in this chapter.

What are you carrying?

In an earlier chapter, we introduced the concept that each of us is a range of experiences, good and bad, from our life journey thus far and within this, your formative years have a significant impact. As much as we might like to think we can separate our work and personal dimensions, both aspects inform who we are and how we respond in certain situations.

This compilation of experiences is carried within us and those difficult and traumatic experiences that are not yet processed, are the heaviest items of luggage. These are the painful events that we've decided (consciously or otherwise) that we can't yet look at or acknowledge. We've not been able to confront these truths, which also means we haven't yet absorbed the learnings.

When we've processed a difficult event, we can acknowledge and accept it as part of our narrative. We can integrate it into the history line. We don't necessarily need to agree with what happened or the consequences thereof, but if we can acknowledge it happened and include it, we are less exposed to emotional hijacking as you'll see in the example below. That said, it is only appropriate to lean into these areas, with support, when you are ready to unpack the layers and do 'your own work'.

Within a team setting, when things are not unpacked, confronted, and acknowledged, they stick to the edges of the team's consciousness and absorb energy. Consequently, individuals within the team (and sometimes the team as a whole) are holding the issue quietly to 'one side'. This is not helpful and will dilute and often destroy the energy that is available for the current context.

That which is excluded has the most power in the system.

My own experience of realising I had some unfinished business to attend to surfaced when I was confronted by a difficult work relationship. It had been going very well for several years and it felt like a mutually rewarding situation.

However, as is the case with some relationships, the upcoming future was giving me signals that it was time for this relationship to come to an end, to create space for my continued growth and expansion. The relationship was becoming strained and unhealthy, but I was avoiding acting.

At an instinctual level, I knew it was time to bring it to a close, but I continued to try to make it work, without success. It was taking up and draining a lot of my energy. Nevertheless, I was not confronting the truth and my cognitive functioning was clouded by strong emotions.

I reached out for expert help via a systemic coaching session and unpacked the layers. I was shocked to realise that the reason I couldn't face saying goodbye, was very little to do with this particular relationship. The source of the avoidance was that I had not fully grieved the sudden loss of my father. Until I was able to properly say goodbye to him, I was not able to bring closure in other settings.

This is a classic demonstration of the fact that when we exclude something, it holds the power and an example of the context overlay pattern referenced in Chapter 7.

Just as your team members may be carrying limiting patterns from their trajectory thus far, it's important to create the space for some deeper exploration of your own. You can't change your past but with appropriate systemic intervention, you can shift your inner relationship with it. Even from the most challenging experiences, you will be able to harvest insights and learnings.

The investment in deepening your self-awareness and really understanding your own patterns and your triggers is a vital component of leadership development.

Patterns Attract Patterns

Be alert to the phenomenon that patterns attract patterns. This can be both positive and negative. If one of your patterns is being a ripe candidate to fill a void in the levels above, then be aware that you are very likely to be attracted to a role where there is a strong likelihood of this. There is also a strong chance that you will have an unconscious bias for team members who are also prone to this pattern.

If you are constantly pulled away and 'sucked up' to the next level, you will leave a void behind you. This will create triangulation within your own team and is not a healthy dynamic if it is sustained over a protracted period. In fact, it is very likely to create hidden tensions and will weaken the team in the longer term.

Finding Your Optimum Place in the Team

As the leader of the team, you will feel drawn into various positions. Occasionally, it will be important to lead from the front, sometimes from behind and when required, you will need to shift to a position alongside the team. The provocation in this chapter is to pause and ask yourself – is this a conscious choice OR a result of your default mode and influenced by your natural preferences?

The business environment we currently find ourselves in i.e., a global landscape of increasing complexity, accelerated pace and expectations of development, exponential digitalisation, and the unknown ingredient of AI, does not make this an easy decision.

In the same way that the team purpose provides some anchorage, as we discovered in Chapter 6, so is the case with the position of the leader. There is a delicate balance of providing this anchorage whilst at the same time acknowledging that your team may have more expertise in the challenge at hand than you.

As we covered earlier, the hierarchy of place, time and expertise is complex and there will be multiple layers operating simultaneously. This makes it even more crucial that you are aware of your own purpose as a leader i.e., beyond the team purpose as you'll see in the following client example. From this dimension of clarity, you will be able to distinguish your right place.

Archetypal Set Up Of A Leadership Team

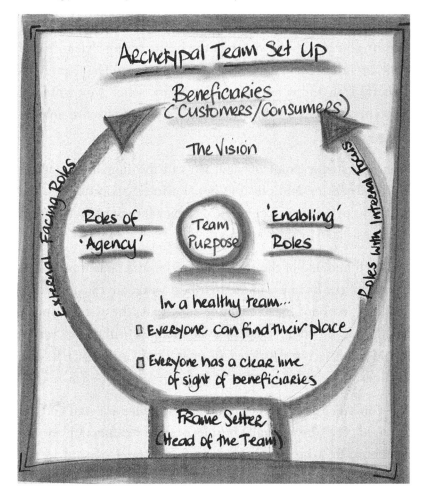

From a systemic perspective, there is an optimum place for the leader of the team to settle. This positions leaders to 'hold the whole'. They are influenced and anchored by the team purpose and vision but also maintain the focus on the external landscape and those that are served by the team.

The visual above illustrates the archetypal set-up of a leadership team, whereby the frame setter for the system (the head of the team) is at the position of '6 o'clock', facing the purpose of the team/business with the vision of the business and a clear line of sight to the customers/clients/beneficiaries. The optimum scenario is that to either side of the 'frame setter', you will have two types of functions based on the roles they enact in and for the system.

From a systemic point of view, we call the functions that are externally facing and creating new business opportunities, the functions of 'agency'. Examples of agency functions include, but is not restricted to, sales and marketing.

On the other side of the frame setter, the functions that enable the rest of the business to do their best work, are categorised as enablers. Without these enabling functions, the system simply would not function. Examples of enabling functions would include, but is not restricted to operations, logistics, HR, and facilities.

The combination of agency and enabling roles are vital and are required for the overall business/team to function at its optimum. In a healthy system, each role (and person) in the team understands where it fits and how it contributes, and there is mutual respect of each other's efforts. Everyone understands where and how decisions are made and what needs to be escalated versus what can sit within the scope of the individual roles.

In a healthy team: Everyone can find their place
AND
Has a clear line of sight of the ultimate beneficiary

This archetypal form also ensures:

- Everyone has a clear line of sight to the customers/clients/beneficiaries
- All roles have a clear and equal sense of place, regardless of their function
- Each role feels valued for its contribution to the purpose and to the beneficiary
- There is an equal share of voice when it comes to decision-making.
- The frame setter holds the whole

This archetypal team set-up is relevant for any team, regardless of where it is in the hierarchy of the organisation – the same principles can be applied.

———

Let's pick up on the example of Shivaun, whom we introduced in Chapter 4. She had inherited her boss' role of Global CEO of a highly successful organisation and, as described earlier, she took some time to help the team hit the 'reset' button.

The first step in this process was incorporating the 'healthy endings' intervention with her line manager to ensure systemic ownership of the team was hers to take, as described in Chapter 5. From there, she dedicated space to acknowledge, honour and celebrate all that was experienced and achieved with the previous CEO at the helm. This embraced the first H of the 3 x H framework – honouring history, described in Chapter 3.

She was intentional about the tone and climate she wanted to create from the outset. She consciously created an environment of honesty, openness and transparency and brought a genuine level of humility to the conversation. All of this set the foundations for psychological safety, and she still receives feedback one year on that this was a turning point in the quality of conversations at the leadership table.

An additional dimension that Shivaun thought long and hard about, was where she wanted to 'place' herself in the team. She was clear that she was a very different leader to her predecessor and wanted to create the space to contemplate and share this thinking with the team. After the honouring history piece (where they acknowledged and celebrated the previous CEO) as outlined in Chapter 3, they took some time to look at the present context and opened conversations about how everyone felt, both generally and regarding this transition in leadership.

To help initiate this, they 'mapped the system' and their respective roles within it as described in Chapter 8. The tensions and some confusion between roles soon emerged and provided the platform for healthy conversation.

In addition, it became very clear where the predecessor had placed themselves in the team and where they were heavily reliant on their CEO for operating from that position. Shivaun was clear that she wanted to operate from a different place and by adjusting this, to an image closer to the archetypal visual above, she created the conditions for the team to be less dependent on her and feel more empowered. She wanted to fully leverage their expertise and experience.

Shivaun led the way and role-modelled the level of honesty, transparency that she wanted to evoke in the team. They shared their hopes, fears, expectations, and questions. Shivaun declared that nothing was 'off the table' and that she would listen and take time to figure out what was needed moving forward.

This is a great example of shifting from honouring the history, to creating the environment for honesty (as per the 3 x H framework introduced in Chapter 3).

Resourcing Yourself

We started this chapter with the theme of energy, so it feels wholly appropriate to come back to this theme in the context of how you are taking care of and refuelling yourself.

How are you looking after your own energy sources? Do you notice what tops you up and what drains you? Are you aware of what triggers your nervous system and have you got practices in place to re-ground yourself and to find your centre?

What we know from a systemic perspective is that when you are centred and you can acknowledge and incorporate all the resources behind you, especially your ancestry, you are more able to fully take and own your optimum place in the system.

You will have preferences on what works for you, but here is an overview of some practices that have been proven to have significant benefits.

Journaling

The practice of journaling is not only therapeutic and a productive way to capture your thoughts, but it also provides a confidential space for you to start noticing patterns. The act of writing them down creates some literal distance from the issues concerned and facilitates an inner spaciousness. This distance allows more perspective on stressful scenarios that, in turn, makes way for constructive processing.

Journaling is known to improve well-being and to also be a memory booster. In today's ever-increasing pace of business, it creates a discipline of reflection and the conditions where the best ideas are more likely to emerge.

If you don't currently journal, try it as a weekly practice and ideally build up to a daily routine. I can personally endorse this as one of the most effective ways to stay grounded, clear and in tune with yourself – the foundations for resonance with others.

Movement

It is often said that the best ideas won't come when you're at your desk. This is also true in terms of regulating your nervous system. You might need to come offline.

As mentioned earlier, there is a strong connection between your body and your brain. It might be helpful to instigate some movement, especially when you are in the middle of a tense period or a complex conundrum. Allow some oxygen into the situation – literally and metaphorically. It will positively shift your mood and open new neural pathways for fresh thinking.

Consider how you can incorporate daily practices of movement for yourself. It might be a walk before work, maybe in between meetings or perhaps over your lunch break. Bear in mind, though, it doesn't need to be separate from the team.

Have a think about how you might be able to weave this healthy practice into the team agenda. For example, carving up some time for buddying up in pairs where conversations can be taken outside. Not every team conversation needs to be around a desk or on a screen.

Maybe even introduce this as a ritual within your face-to-face meetings. Find a way to carve up the agenda so that walking conversations become a regular fixture. How can you proactively shift the energy within your team on a regular basis?

Meditation

Meditation in its purest form isn't for everyone but there are lots of ways to evoke a meditative state, such as yoga, Thai chi, painting, drawing or being with animals. Find your way of instilling some zen in your life. It's worth remembering that five minutes every day will probably have a bigger impact than an hour each week.

Quality Sleep

This is probably one of the most underrated practices and yet, one of the most essential. If you haven't read it already, I'd strongly recommend the book 'Why We Sleep' by Matthew Walker. As an alternative, you can check out his Ted talk.

Let's say it as it is. Sleep is critically important – ignore this at your peril. It is literally life changing. The right proportion nurtures our mental well-being, enables improved brain function, and helps mitigate chronic illness.

Research has shown that those who consistently get less than an average of seven hours of sleep per night have a 26% higher chance of dying prematurely. Each of us needs a different quota of sleep but just because you've got into a routine of surviving on fewer hours doesn't necessarily mean that's the optimum ratio for your physical and mental well-being.

You may have alternative ways of resourcing yourself and if you don't, may I suggest you experiment to discover what works for you. I don't think any of us would disagree that when we are well-rested, feeling good in our bodies, clear in our minds and feeling more grounded, we can bring out the best of ourselves.

Some of the most successful teams have shared practices that enable the entire team to re-ground themselves and orient on what's vitally important at that moment. One of these is the quality check-in process, which is available in the resources section, Chapter 12.

In summary, taking some time to look inwards will reap exponential benefits for you and for your team. As the book title suggests, don't be surprised to discover that the team is NOT the issue. There is a range of key elements that you can proactively address and practically apply that can make the difference between a leadership role that flows and gives you joy OR feels like heavy lifting and 'treading treacle'.

Percolations

- What few words would you love your team to spontaneously use, to describe:

  o YOU
  o Their experience of your leadership

- If the words above, don't reflect your current reality – what might this be telling you?

  o About your impact?
  o About the patterns you might be carrying?
  o Where do these come from?
  o What are they trying to communicate?
  o What situations/triggers have the potential to hijack you if you are not mindful?

- What is your purpose as the leader of this team?

- Bearing that in mind, what is your optimum position for you in relation to the team?

- How do you take care of your own energy?

  ○ How do you resource yourself to bring the best version of yourself to the team?

- What does the team need from YOU to be at their best?

- Taking all of that into consideration, what needs your attention right now?

11

AN OPEN SYSTEM NEEDS TO EVOLVE

To progress and thrive, a system needs to remain open. It needs to have a permeable membrane, such that it can attune to the market and the evolving needs of those it serves. If this membrane is too thick, it weakens the signals from the external context. The net result is that the organisation will lag in terms of its responsiveness, relevance and therefore also its competitiveness.

If the membrane of the system is too thick, the impulses for change won't get through.

From a systemic perspective, the evolutionary force of the upcoming future is constantly coming towards us. The challenge for leadership is to ensure the organisation can move and align with this energy of continuous renewal.

This evolutionary force, however, also challenges us to consider what needs to come to an end. To create space for the new, it asks us:

What has reached its destiny and is ready to come to an end?

Within business and beyond, we are conditioned to believe that it is important to have a plan, to operate with intentionality and to drive clarity through every layer of the organisation. This is certainly one of the components of success but is generally purely driven by a cognitive and logical mindset and is often informed by ego.

The evolutionary force of the upcoming future has more of a feeling of fate or destiny – meaning it is happening anyway and our challenge is to receive the signals and find a way to optimise the flow of this life force. From a systemic perspective, therefore, an additional success criteria, is the capacity to move in alignment with and respond to this evolutionary force. Since it is flowing towards us, and outside of our control, the provocation is to be much more emergent rather than too locked into a 'plan'.

Can your team be more emergent or are you locked into 'the plan'?

This evolutionary force of the upcoming future is as relevant at the individual dimension as it is for a team and the organisation as a whole. It is a very relevant and insightful process to incorporate in a development session with your team. Bear in mind that you might need to support them and create the conditions of readiness for the next step.

Generally, there is lots of energy, excitement, and appetite for launching and the introduction of new concepts, products, and services to the market. There is much less energy and attention applied to the discipline of discerning what has reached its destiny and usefulness. This is as relevant to products and services as it is to the architecture of the organisation and the roles within it.

Reviewing the organisation is often a purely cognitive and logical process and undertaken in line with a strategic review process at set times in the calendar. The frequency will range from team to team and will be informed by the wider organisational rhythm. In principle, this is, at most, a quarterly undertaking.

One of the ways in which the systemic approach can be practically applied is to also bring more of an instinctive and embodied perspective. As is it much less time intensive and requires less preparation time, it can also be introduced more frequently.

This is an incredibly powerful process to deploy in the formation stages of the team and can also immediately surface any areas of tension, challenge, and opportunity.

This is applied via a 3D mapping process, whereby the team are challenged with the task of identifying all the key components that need to be incorporated to illustrate their context. This will include, but is not limited to the following:

- Vision of the Organisation
- Organisation/team purpose
- Those served by the team/organisation
- The ecosystem within which these beneficiaries reside
- Suppliers/Strategic Partners
- Competitors
- Other key factors and events in the external context e.g., key initiatives such as the drive for sustainability

There is no limit to the number of elements included. The focus is more on making it real and relevant. The brief is to create a map that represents the current reality of the team/organisation and the various conditions and factors that are active (or are coming over the horizon).

Each element is represented simply by a piece of A4 paper – or if you want to create a more dynamic picture that represents the scale and texture of the context, you could use also incorporate other materials such as cardboard boxes or objects.

The process entails two rounds of 'mapping':

Round One

Round one is to invite the team to 'map' each of the elements in terms of how they are situated in relationship with each other. Ask them to pay attention to proximity and distance, and to what is paying attention to what. The first draft of the map aims to represent the AS IS position, i.e., the current reality as they see it and sense it. It is critical that the team are encouraged to place each element by tapping into their intuition and their gut instinct as referenced earlier.

They will be tempted to set up the map as they think it 'should be', not least because this embodied dimension of knowledge is utilised less often. It is the real picture i.e., the As Is map that will give you access to the hidden layers within the system.

When this first draft is complete, invite the team to step back so that they can see the map as a whole system. Invite their observations.

Has the system got the capacity and space to evolve?

Here are a few examples of precision questions that will provoke insights:

- What is the level of energy in this system?

  º Where specifically, do you sense vitality & the capacity to move?
  º Where is there a sense of being stuck, stagnant or toxicity?

- What specifically isn't in a good place (yet)?

- What tensions are you noticing and what is underneath these?

  º What symptoms are you noticing?
  º If the system could speak – what would it be trying to convey?

- If we aren't looking forward, what are we pre-occupied with?

- How would you assess our capacity to evolve?

Round Two

When the reflections have had some time to be heard and received, invite the team into Round Two, to update the 'map' so that it depicts a healthier and more vibrant version.

Give them plenty of time to nuance the adjustments but also give voice to their embodied knowledge of what needs to move and why.

Resist the temptation to challenge any moves but instead, bring more curiosity to the conversation. Help them articulate what they sense is over the horizon and how the team might respond to this.

Give space to the classic interactions and jostling between certain parts and/or roles within the team. It will take time for each member of the team to find their place within this new set-up.

As you observe the iterations emerging, bear in mind the principles behind the archetypal set-up of a healthy team. The following provocations will be helpful as the team continue to nuance the map:

- Has everyone got a line of sight to those we serve?
- What is our team purpose and how does it help anchor us?

- Can everyone find their place in the team?
- What needs to be adjusted so that everyone understands how they contribute to our vision and our purpose?

Allow for various iterations until the whole team finally settles on a version that they are comfortable with and are aligned behind. When this has had time to be shared and understood, you can then transition into a more cognitive dimension and generate a plan for what this means and how to make it happen.

This process of opening the team to the movement that was needed, was successfully deployed in the following client example.

Let's come back to Issac, the new CEO of a family-owned business, one final time.

Issac gathered his leadership team together to face a challenging landscape. Organic growth was shrinking, and market conditions meant that significant transformation was required, both in terms of how they brought their product to market and how they organised themselves internally. A key component of this was the need for digital transformation.

He had inherited his leadership team and most of them had been in the organisation for some time. Several systemic interventions were incorporated in these formative stages of the team's development. They started by mapping and honouring the history of the two founding organisations that had come together via acquisition some twelve years earlier. The integration had not been easy. The host organisation did not feel appreciated for rescuing the other organisation from a sale process that was downgrading its value, and the acquired organisation did not feel valued for its creativity and its track record for innovative launches.

Instead of feeling integrated, the organisations felt more like they were running alongside each other. This was also the case with the associated teams. The lack of acknowledgement and appreciation of this period was showing up as a splitting dynamic in lots of areas and created a polarising effect in the team, as referenced in Chapter 7.

The system, in its drive for completeness, was continually surfacing this split and the associated dynamics. It was prompting the organisation to confront and acknowledge the difficulty so that it could be explicitly included within the narrative.

The loss and the shedding of brands, friends and colleagues were fully acknowledged. The sacrifices and the survivor's guilt were also acknowledged. When all of this could be seen and fully included in the narrative, the required level of settling, meaningful understanding and trust-building could begin.

Following on from the work of fully acknowledging the history, the team moved to the next stage of the 3X H framework and embraced the philosophy of being honest about where they were as a business.

They embraced this by mapping out the hidden architecture of their wider ecosystem. This physical 3D map that represented the current system was developed gradually by the team. They included all functions, the customers, consumers, and the owners.

Although the organisation was developing brilliant products and services for its ultimate consumer, it became abundantly apparent that most of the functions (and the teams within them) were mostly focussing on the owners of the business rather than facing the customers and consumers. It also became clear that the energy in this system was contained and stifled.

This helped the leadership team realise that the purpose that was being lived was predominately more internally driven and, facing towards the owners rather than the evolving dynamics in the marketplace.

Their predominately inward-facing trajectory meant that they were much less responsive to a rapidly changing environment. It was a 'closed system' and was therefore becoming more exposed in terms of the long-term success of the business. They were not currently set up to respond to a rapidly evolving marketplace.

These uncomfortable truths may have surfaced over time through conversation, but the intensity of the realisation was significantly increased by the presence of a physical 3D map right in front of the team, within the space.

Round Two

The team moved on to round two and developed their 'map' to the next stage. They were invited to adjust the set-up to represent an organisation that was more connected to their consumer and customers, with a capacity to respond to their evolving needs.
Having established a more robust connection with those they served, they turned their attention to the internal architecture of the system, and how they could be in relation with each other so that cohesion and vitality were instilled.

The resulting map was a dramatically different picture from the first iteration and correlated to the reshaping of the business that followed. This reshaped map also clarified, in a very tangible way, the purpose of the organisation and that of the leadership team in terms of their role in driving the required transformation.

This leadership team moved from being a fragmented set of experienced leaders, slightly sceptical of a new CEO and predominately operating from their separate silos to a cohesive team of leaders, driving an aligned agenda of transformation, who had each other's backs.

This 3D mapping process can be deployed at any stage of the team's development. It is ideal to incorporate it at the formative stages of the team and produce a baseline that the team can continually review.

It is also a particularly helpful process to incorporate whilst discerning the team purpose. It offers a much more embodied intelligence to this process and can significantly speed up clarity, cohesion, and energetic alignment.

12

FINAL PERCOLATIONS & RESOURCES

Percolations are intended to support your reflections as a leader. I encourage you to spend a few minutes capturing your thoughts and ideas that emerge. If it feels right, these musings might be worth bringing to one of your team development sessions as a platform for a rich conversation.

- Where are your team currently in terms of moving through the forming and storming stages?

- How could you integrate the systemic principles outlined, to help move the team towards the potential you know is possible?

- How psychologically safe does the team feel to bring issues to the collective environment?

- How clear is the team on their purpose?

- If you were to visualise how the team currently occupy their roles, how would it compare to the archetypal optimum shape of a team, shared in Chapter 10?

- What systemic patterns might be vibrating in the system and how are they impacting your team?

- When you pause to look beneath this, what might they be a solution for?

- How might you create the conditions so that these can be surfaced and worked through?

- How might the 3 x H framework be helpful for your team and where you are on the journey together?

- What's the one thing that YOU can do (in terms of your leadership) that will make a positive difference?

Resources

CONTENTS LIST

- **Systemic Route Map**

- **Systemic Questions portfolio**

- **Preparation Resources**

  - **Stakeholder Feedback**
  - **Check-in process**

- **Honour History**

  - **History Map**

- **Healthy Endings Process**

- **Systemic Housewarming**

  - **Integrating new members**

- **Archetypal Team set-up**

- **Portfolio of Poems**

Systemic Route Map

The route map below, gives you a 'bird's eye view' of the recommended process of taking your team from stuck, to surfacing the dynamics and the tension, acknowledging their roots and ultimately, facilitating progressive movement. This route map incorporates the overarching systemic process outlined in the previous chapter and the practical application of this via the 3 x H model, as referenced in Chapter 3.

Bear in mind that you might not deploy all stages immediately or in the same session. It might be about unpacking the layers that are ready and then coming back to pick up the rest. Don't underestimate the value of giving the team space to reflect and digest. It's OK to be one step ahead but be mindful of not pushing so hard that you end up creating resistance.

PREPARATION

- Create psychological safety
- Healthy endings
- Systemic Housewarming – integrate new members.

HONOUR HISTORY

- Map the History

  ᵒ Include and acknowledge all of what (and who) has been before

BE HONEST ABOUT THE PRESENT

- Identify the patterns, the root cause, and the pain points.
- Surface the tension and acknowledge what is.
- Pattern release – harvest insights and learnings

CREATE HOPE FOR THE FUTURE

- Mapping the context – landscape scanning

- Let the team purpose emerge

- Agree a clear flow of leadership

  o Let everyone take their place (relative to the purpose)
  o Contract on mutual exchange between members
  o Clarify ways of working, including decision making
  o Agree a rhythm & cadence of coming together that enables agility & flow

MAINTAIN MOMENTUM

- Revisit and refresh the purpose in context of the evolving market.

- Take time to reflect on what the team needs from YOU – not the other way around

Systemic Questions Portfolio

Please find below, a portfolio of systemic questions that will encourage you to stay curious and look beyond the surface layers of a situation with your team. This is not an exhaustive list but a good place to start building your muscle.

Bear in mind that one of the essential ingredients in effective listening, is to cut through the noise and listen in an embodied way. Your body is a highly attuned sensing device – use it!

Stay curious and keep asking yourself, when I listen beyond the words – what additional insights are being revealed?

- How long has this issue/pattern/dynamic been happening?

- Where else is this happening in the wider organisation?

- What is the system trying to communicate through this issue/problem or repeating pattern?

  o Could it be something to do with belonging or not belonging?
  o Does it have something to do with clarity or security of place?
  o Or perhaps about the balance of giving and taking?
  o What is it that we may have been avoiding and need to see/confront and remember?

- What could be the very good reason for this repeating pattern?

- What is the systemic function of this dynamic – i.e., what is it trying to do for the system?

- What needs to be acknowledged?

- What is the unmet need of this person, this role, or the wider system?

- Where can we see the potential for movement?

These questions are applicable at any stage of the systemic process.

Preparation Resources: Stakeholder Feedback

Some members of your team might not yet be comfortable to speak their truth in the collective space. In addition, you need to create room for all sorts of preferences so that you can demonstrate genuine inclusively. Stay open to gathering insight from the team in advance of pulling them into a development session. This enables you to meet them where they are at and to gradually accelerate the process of unpacking the layers that need attention.

The following series of questions are suggested areas to explore either via a questionnaire or conversationally with each member of your team in advance. You can do this directly with your team or get some resource (internal or external) to create a confidential space for the feedback to be gathered and collated anonymously.

Gathering Stakeholder Feedback in Advance of a Team Session

Proposed Qualitative Questions:

- What is happening in this team that is ADDING VALUE?

- What is happening in this team (even if it is unconsciously) that might be DILUTING VALUE?

  ᵒ Identify an example of this aspect and potentially ask for more than one example to check if it's a 'one-off' scenario
  ᵒ Check how long this dynamic has been active, with a particular curiosity about when the dynamic started.

- What needs to happen in the forthcoming team session for it to add real value, from your perspective?

  ᵒ Explore how they will know or sense this value – they will have an internal barometer or way of knowing what is helpful to bring to the surface
  ᵒ Explore what will happen and what won't happen if the forthcoming team session is a valuable intervention

The next set of proposed questions are quantitative and are helpful for giving you a sense of the scale of the gap between the perceived starting point and the ideal.

Proposed Quantitative Questions

The range of scores for each of these is 1-10, whereby 10 = the healthiest end of the scale.

- To what degree is there clarity and alignment on the sense of purpose of the team?
- To what degree can each member/part of the team find and fully occupy their place in the team?
- To what degree is there a healthy sense of mutual exchange (a balance of give and take over time)
- To what degree is there a sense of belonging in the team?

It is recommended that the stakeholder feedback is consolidated into themes and shared with the team in advance, together with the headline agenda.

This transparency is part of the process of creating a safe container and provides everyone with the opportunity to reflect and prepare for meaningful conversation.

The stakeholder conversations are likely to give you very tangible examples of symptoms and behaviours. Your challenge is not to get sucked in by these but to dig deeper, identify the patterns and ultimately surface the root cause of those dynamics.

PREPARATION RESOURCES

Check-In Processes

AT THE START OF A SESSION

Check-in conversations are designed to get everyone's voices in the room as early as possible and to get a sense of how the team are genuinely arriving (what state of mind they are in).

It's helpful to go beyond the cliches. Invite and encourage the team to delve beneath the surface layer when they check in. Ask them to share in the broadest sense, i.e., as a whole person. It is recommended that you send a brief in advance to create the space for appropriate preparation.

The brief below enables a glimpse of the personal system of each person to be included.

Please come prepared to share the following:

- When we bring our full selves, it's a much richer and deeper experience of getting to know each other. We invite you to share an essence (glimpse) of your heritage and personal system, by finishing the following sentence:

  ○ "I come from 'a tribe', who..."

- Your place in the team (your role, when you arrived AND what you bring with you into your role, including experience from this organisation and beyond)

- Something that you're proud of from the past twelve months. This could be:

  ○ A significant piece of work
  ○ Progress delivered by your area/function/market
  ○ Something personal to you and your leadership

- What are your hopes, fears, and expectations for the period (year, quarter, month) ahead?

- What would make this a valuable session for you?

  ○ And how will you know?

PARTWAY THROUGH A SESSION

It can be helpful to undertake a 'temperature check' part way through a session to assess how the team are feeling and responding. Staying attuned to what's working and what's needed will help you ensure you are getting beneath the veneer.

Here are a few suggested questions you can utilise to provoke another level of conversation:

- If we zoom back beyond the specifics, what do you sense is really going on here?

○ When did this start and what might be the very good reason for this?
○ What is this telling us?
○ And if we zoom back further, what do you believe this team needs at this stage?

- What is it that we are not yet looking at/seeing that is vital to help us get to the next level?

- What are you picking up that need's attention?

A quality check out is also important!

Honouring History
HISTORY MAP – CREATING YOUR HISTORY TIMELINE
(1 of 2)

This is one of the most powerful and inclusive interventions and is highly interactive and energising for a team. It is one of the formative stages in the systemic process and helps you uncover what work is needed to free the team up for optimum vitality and exceptional performance.

Objectives

- Ensures that all events, milestones, and contributors are included and where appropriate, remembered in the narrative (this directly addresses exclusion)
- Pinpoints pain points and potential traumas that have not been confronted so that the appropriate interventions can be incorporated

Process – 3 x key phases

Phase 1:

- Involve the team in creating a 'history wall' i.e., a multi-faceted visual that includes all that has happened up to the current time (see team brief below)
- Go as far back as feels relevant – sometimes it is appropriate to go as far back as the founders and as a minimum, go back as far as the formation of the team
- It is particularly helpful to incorporate the expert help of a graphic illustrator for this part of the process

Phase 2:

- Invite the team to step back and take it all in
- Encourage them to reflect on and share the key themes and patterns
- Provide gentle provocation to call out what has not, up to this point, been confronted and acknowledged (e.g., pain points that have been avoided)
- Encourage an open conversation about difficulties that have not been processed

Phase 3:

- If appropriate, introduce the appropriate intervention/s that free the team up

  o Bear in mind, the pace and depth the team are ready for
  o Sometimes, phase 1 and 2 is enough if this is the first experience of this approach – you can come back to it next time

It is helpful to create a blank mural in advance and divide this into 3 x categories:

- Key events and milestones
- Key contributors (people)
- Key moments

You may find you need a fourth category, based on what the team come back with.

Honouring History:
CREATING YOUR HISTORY TIMELINE
(2 of 2)

Team Brief:

Create a timeline of how we got to where we are today, including all the key events and people that have helped shape or inform how the team exists today.

Go as far back as the formation of the team and if it feels appropriate, go back to the founding of the organisation.

Include within this timeline:

- Key events and milestones (.launches, divestments etc.)

  o Key events within the industry that have shaped the way we do things

- Changes in the architecture of the team and/or the business, such as restructuring mergers and acquisitions

- Key contributors that have influenced the team and organisation we are today

  o Include key leaders AND unsung heroes

- Difficult moments

- ○ Especially those that may have been forgotten/avoided/we don't talk about
- ○ Painful experiences

- Breakthrough moments

- Significant memories

- Key celebrations

Healthy Endings Process (1 Of 2)

When is this relevant?

This systemic intervention can be utilised when something is coming to an end and to 'free people' up to move towards their own upcoming future (and detach from that which is ending). Within a team context, it would be relevant to support employees to detach in a healthy way following restructuring, the closure of brands or a business identity, and when organisations are divesting parts of the business.

This is also relevant on an individual basis, for example, when a leader is leaving their team/role/function/organisation. In both cases, it is recommended that this process is facilitated so that the individual/the whole team can be fully IN the process.

Objectives of Intervention:

INDIVIDUAL PIECE: To enable an individual to bring all of themselves with them into their next role/adventure and to leave behind that which will no longer belongs to them (clarifying systemic ownership). This enables their successor to fully occupy their new responsibility and to have the freedom to pick things up and develop them as they see fit.

TEAM PIECE: To release the team energetically from something they have been heavily involved with and invested in. To ensure they fully detach from something significant, thereby creating some capacity for the new. If the work that is being concluded is moving to others, then it is important to clarify that systemic ownership is moving and the existing team have no further claim to the ongoing development.

Phase One – Preparation and Logistics

What you need:

- Object/symbol to represent 'other' (organisation, role, function, person who is assuming ownership)
- Markers (e.g., pieces of paper) for <u>each element</u> of what was contributed AND will stay with 'the other', without any further claims on the part of the individual/team
- Markers for each element which the individual/team needs to reclaim i.e., parts of themselves, their energy, their spirit plus any IP which is <u>legitimately</u> theirs.

Once all the 'elements' are identified, and markers/objects/symbols created/established – invite the group (or individual) to ground/centre themselves for a few moments. This can be as simple as taking a few deep breaths and a moment of silence.

Phase Two – Facilitating the Intervention

1. Invite the individual/team to decide their orientation for past, present, and future AND invite them to place a marker for the 'other' (e.g., Organisation) with that architecture of time in mind.

2. Ask them to place the collection markers that represent what they will need to reclaim in a pile beside the marker for 'other' – you will come back to them later.

3. Get them to pick up each element that represents what was given and can stay with the 'other', ONE MARKER AT A TIME.

4. With each marker/symbol, give the script below for the individual/team to say (out loud or within themselves) as they

place each item BESIDE the marker for 'other. Feel free to fine-tune some of the wording to fit their context (and they may wish to do that for themselves).

Healthy Endings Process (2 Of 2)

Script for each element that is being placed by the marker for the 'other':

"This is what I gave you/contributed. I gave it willingly and with dedication/love/good intention/as part of my role of xxxxx (allow the client to use whichever phrase resonates the most). You can do with it whatever is appropriate – I have no further claim to this." (If it is a team piece, replace I with WE.)

5. When all elements that need to be fully given back, without claim have been given to the 'other', shift to those elements that need to be reclaimed.

6. Ask the individual/team to pick up the markers that represent that which needs to be reclaimed (parts of themselves) ONE AT A TIME

7. As each one is picked up – ask them to repeat the script below (out loud or within themselves)

Script for each element that is being reclaimed from the 'other':

"I also gave you xxxxx (e.g., passion and creativity) – this is part of me, and I need it/these to step into the rest of my life/career/journey (whichever is relevant). I will take this with me." (Replace WE and US, instead of I, as required.)

8. Invite the individual/team to fully reconnect with each element that is being reclaimed BEFORE moving on to the next.

9. When all elements have been reclaimed – invite them to look at each one as they are holding them, then turn towards their

upcoming future AND take a step towards it, with the reclaimed markers in hand.

10. Invite them to sense what they are stepping away from fully AND what they are taking with them and if it feels right, invite them to take a further step towards their upcoming future.

Depending on the context and setting, a powerful way to close could be by way of a fire ceremony/ritual whereby the elements that are being given back to 'other' are put into the fire. This symbolises the giving back and leaving it up to the other (the fire) as to what it wants to do with them.

This exercise was originally inspired by Jan Jacob Stam and further developed by the author Tess Cope

Systemic Housewarming – Integrating New Team Members

The 'systemic housewarming process' is a way of integrating new team members and providing a pause to review ways of thinking, working, and relating.

Objectives:

- Creates psychological safety in small groups
- Identifies what's working/not working (including repeating patterns) through various lenses
- Ensures all voices are heard and included
- Highlights where there is space for new thinking, underlines what wants to be continued and identifies what is ready to end.
- Enables new starters to know that their seat is fully available and that they are welcome to bring their full selves into the role.

It is recommended that the team is split into groups, based on years of experience, and given some time to reflect and meaningfully discuss, before bringing their thoughts to the wider team.

See the following suggestions below:

Group 1: Less than 1 year

Group 2: 1 -3 years

Group 3:3 years +

Recommended Brief

Group 1

- What are the obvious areas of opportunity you can see in the ways of working as a team?
- What ideas/concepts would you like to bring to the team (from your experience), if the team is open to them?

Group 2

- What do you enjoy about working in this team?
- What are the repeating patterns that keep coming up that you'd like to explore, unpack, and move beyond?
- What are the unresolved issues that you'd like to table?
- What decisions need to be revisited?

Group 3

- What are the areas that work well, and you're invested in maintaining?
- What's the glue that makes it work?
- What are you open to/what are the areas of opportunity?

This exercise was originally inspired by Jan Jacob Stam and further developed by the author Tess Cope

Archetypal Leadership Team Set-Up:

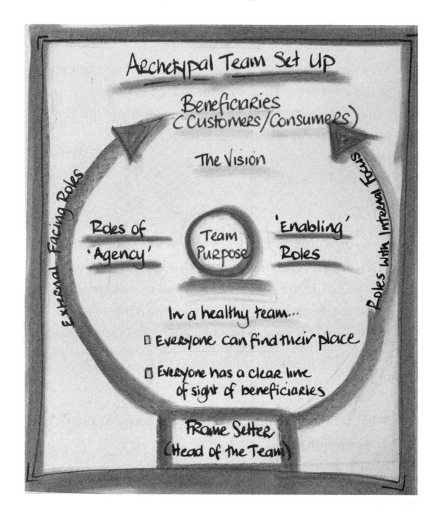

The visual above illustrates the archetypal setup of an effective team, whereby the frame setter for the system (the head of the team) is at the position of '6 o'clock', facing the purpose of the team/business with the vision of the business and a clear line of sight to the customers/clients/beneficiaries. The optimum scenario, as illustrated in the visual below, is that to either side of the 'frame setter', you will have two types of roles or functions based on what they do for the system.

From a systemic point of view, we call those functions that are externally facing and creating new business opportunities, the functions of 'agency'. Examples of agency functions include but are not limited to, sales and marketing.

On the other side of the frame setter (the head of the team), the functions that enable the rest of the business to do their best work, are categorised as enablers. Without these enabling functions, the system simply would not function. Examples of enabling functions would include but are not limited to, operations, logistics, HR, and facilities.

The combination of agency and enabling roles are vital and are required for the overall business/team to function at its optimum. In a healthy system, each role (and person) in the team understands where it fits and how it contributes and there is mutual respect for each other's efforts. Everyone understands where and how decisions are made and what needs to be escalated versus what can sit within the scope of the individual roles/functions.

In a healthy team: Everyone can find their place
AND
Has a clear line of sight of the ultimate beneficiary

This archetypal form also ensures:

- Everyone has a clear line of sight to the customers/clients/beneficiaries

- All roles have a clear and equal sense of place, regardless of their function
- Each role feels valued for its contribution to the purpose and to the beneficiary
- There is an equal share of voice when it comes to decision-making.
- The frame setter holds the whole

This archetypal team set-up is relevant for any team, regardless of where it is in the hierarchy of the organisation – the same principles can be applied.

POEMS FOR GROUNDING THE TEAM & TO SUPPORT A SHIFT IN ENERGY (1)

The following portfolio of poems is offered as a way of opening a team session or shifting the energy partway through a session. Poems can set the tone, create spaciousness to calm the nervous system and when appropriate, diffuse tension.

The Truth Of What Is

The truth of what is
Cuts through the noise.
It requires straight lines
And straight talking.

The truth of what is
Can be the most painful,
And the most healing.

The truth of what is
Requires the courage and precision
Of the surgeon's scalpel,
With the deep care of the midwife
To open the wound.

When the truth of what is
Can be fully seen and acknowledged,
Fresh oxygen is allowed in,
The system can breathe
And vitality can return.

TESS COPE – OCTOBER 2021

**POEMS FOR GROUNDING THE TEAM & TO SUPPORT A
SHIFT IN ENERGY (2)
OUR ROOTS
WITHOUT YOU – THIS WOULD NOT BE POSSIBLE**

Far behind me – but not forgotten,
Buried deep but sneaking to the surface
From time to time
Memories of piercing pain and trauma,
Of the internal separation - dividing myself to survive
Talking without communicating
Staying close... to fiercely protect
And having each other's back.
Longing for silence and safety
Amidst the chaos,
Words are not required.

Yet the memories of precious moments
And gatherings to mark the milestones, too many to
      count,
Are also sitting there
Beneath the surface – ready to be seen.
The music, the banter, and the nonstop dancing
And bear hugs, belly laughter and tears of joy.

But I need to survive – it is too intense.
I need to breathe more easily – I try to cut if off,
I try to leave it all behind me – to find my way in
      the dark
But the 'I' and 'US' get lost in the process.

Now here I am - looking back
Only to realise all of this belongs:
From the pain, the gift of real connection
From the trauma, experience of understanding
From the heart, the bigger why.
Each has played its part.
They have informed who I am – and how I walk in
*   the world.*
Without all of this – today would not be possible.
Forever included. Forever grateful.

TESS COPE, NOVEMBER 2022

POEMS FOR GROUNDING THE TEAM & TO SUPPORT A SHIFT IN ENERGY (3)

The Stone In My Shoe

The stone in my shoe is there as a constant.
It rubs my skin from time to time
and it hurts.

The stone in my shoe is there as a constant.
Sometimes it finds a new spot to settle into
And is quiet for a while - not stirring
Until things are triggered, and then it makes itself
*   known.*

To be looked at - to be seen - and to be felt
And when I can acknowledge its presence,
and the gifts I have gained from carrying it,
It can soften and melt back into the background
To become part of the fabric as opposed to separate
*   from it,*

No longer rubbing - but still present.
No longer hurting - but still present.
I honour this stone in my shoe.
It has made me who I am and informed how I walk in
*   the world.*
I am stronger for it - and I would be incomplete
*   without it.*
It has become part of me - and I part of it.
I stand more complete.

And yet, by acknowledging its part - I can also stand
    separate from it,
To look beyond the stone,
To honour the rock from which it was birthed,
The bigger system from which it came.
It is much bigger than me and us,
It too, deserves to be seen.

TESS COPE, MARCH 2019

POEMS FOR GROUNDING THE TEAM & TO SUPPORT A SHIFT IN ENERGY (4)

ONE STEP

*It's too much, too big, too vast - I hear myself say -
  there's so much to do
I need to move fast - to make a leap - I have to jump
My body & mind are all stirred up - I'm getting ready
  to run...*

*But it's too much - it's overwhelming
So I shrink back to where I was and don't move.*

*I'm caught up in the shall I or shall I not?
Time to go OR shall I wait for a while?
I'll wait for the right moment - the sign that it's the
  right time.*

*I'm caught up in illusion of a perfect move
I'm stuck in the vacuum of unused energy, unused
  movement - it's draining me
This polarising pattern of move and don't move yet,
  needs to be released - to be given back.*

*Who owns this?
To whom am I being loyal by keeping this alive
  within me?
And then the mist lifts - there's a bigger context
  beyond me
Where two parts were split*

Where this tussle belongs and makes perfect sense.

And when this can be seen and acknowledged, I'm
    released..
I'm no longer caught up in that 'in between' place
Standing in someone else's shoes
Of wanting to move, but not moving - frozen.

My One Step is a step of the right size - the footprint
    that comes from MY feet
This 'One Step' is not about holding two sides
    separately
or paying a price
It's for me
It's coming from me
It's the right size.

At last, I can breathe
And I can move forward again
One Step at a Time.

TESS COPE

POEMS FOR GROUNDING THE TEAM & TO SUPPORT A SHIFT IN ENERGY (5)
I'M HERE ON YOUR LEFT

I'm here on your left
I'm not too big and,
I won't make you small.
I'm here on your left
So you can stand tall.

I'm here on your left
To be your thought partner,
In whatever form you need.
I'm here on your left
So you can take the lead.

I'm here on your left
To provide the stimulus,
And hold the space.
I'm here on your left
So you can make your decisions
With due consideration and grace.

TESS COPE - 2017

ABOUT THE AUTHOR

Tess is an ICF-accredited leadership coach and team facilitator with over twenty-five years of experience in cultural transformation and leadership development, across a wide range of sectors.

She has held a variety of commercial positions in preparation for her step through to HR roles, which have included Board responsibility. Tess took the plunge to set up The Transformation Agency in 2010 and is actively working with executive leaders and their leadership teams across Europe, the UK, Asia Pac, the US, and the Middle East.

The systemic approach was recommended to Tess as a methodology that helps accelerate real and sustainable transformation back in 2010 and she hasn't looked back since. She has trained with world leaders in this field and has deepened her knowledge and expertise every year since, including her accreditation to bring this approach to organisations.

Tess has integrated this approach throughout her work and has witnessed exponential turnarounds at the organisational, team and individual dimensions.

Her mission is to help leaders improve the working lives of 100,000 employees every year by helping them look beyond the immediate dynamics, unearth the root cause, and move the whole team and wider organisation towards a vibrant, energising, and successful place to work.

Tess and her team spend most of their time working with Leadership Teams around the globe and feel incredibly privileged to offer leadership retreats in the UK and the US.

Beyond the work context, Tess lives in Cambridgeshire, UK with her husband and their menagerie of pets, which include her herd of three horses. On occasion, these three geldings have been known to bring immense value to the coaching process!

If you'd like to get in touch with Tess, you can find her here:

Tess@thetransformationagency.com

https://www.thetransformationagency.com

 linkedin.com/in/tesscope

HOW TO WORK WITH ME

As a leader, I know that you want to get the best out of your team – for them and for the business. I also know that you will have put great effort and investment behind finding the right people for each of the respective roles in your team.

The problems arise when the team are not coming together as a collective force, in the way that you had hoped. Those essential ingredients of capability, character and good intentions at the individual dimension are not stacking up with the behaviours you witness in the team setting.

What makes it even harder, is when you know the tension is going underground and is moving through the layers below. It is not quite visible or explicit enough to grab hold of it, but the impact is corrosive. We understand how frustrating and demoralising this can feel.

From our experience of working with leadership teams across the UK, US, and Europe over the past 13 years, we believe that it's important to zoom back and to look at the situation from a systemic perspective. We can help you with that and would be delighted to be of service.

There are several opportunities to connect, and potentially work together if that feels right.

First and foremost, if you'd like to have an informal call – you can find some time in the diary that works for you here: https://calendly.com/tesscoaching/connect-call-30-mins

Alternatively, we have a significant event coming up in 2023 which might be of interest:

- **6th – 8th December 2023** – We are collaborating with The Systemic Business School of the Netherlands and offering a Systemic Business Leadership Retreat, nr London. You can find more details here: https://thesystemicleadershippretreat.thetransformationagency.com/

If you are more interested in 1:1 Leadership Coaching – please check out this short video with information on our approach - https://vimeo.com/436161438

And if you'd like to discuss the design of a bespoke session for your team, let's have an informal call and we can take it from there. You can find a time that works for you here: https://calendly.com/tesscoaching/connect-call-30-mins

As you may have seen in my bio, my passion is about helping leaders create a positive impact on the working lives of their employees – where people can learn, grow, thrive, and make a meaningful difference in the world through their work. if this resonates – we're on the same page - lets connect.

warmest,

Tess